A journey of healing, connection, and courage

WOVEN
RESILIENCE

REFLECTIONS ON BURNOUT, BALANCE, AND THE POWER OF COMPASSION

Nilam Amin Raval

Published by Inicio Press

https://www.iniciopress.com/

Woven Resilience: Reflections on Burnout, Balance, and the Power of Compassion

ISBN: 978-1-998315-23-9

This book exists because of all of you:

To my daughters—Serena, Kirin, and Layla—who fill my life with love and purpose.

To my beloved Amish—my partner, my anchor, and the heart of every breath I take—this journey is ours.

To my parents, my brother, my sisters-in-law, and my family, whose love, encouragement, and steadfast support have made this possible.

To my peers, my patients, and the dedicated editing and publishing team, who are woven into every page.

We are all threads in this tapestry, and together we have made this book a reality.

Table of Contents

Introduction

As a first-generation American-East Asian woman, I have spent my life discovering my voice and finding my place in a world that often aimed to define me before I could. Raised by hardworking parents who relentlessly supported our family and sponsored relatives to build new lives in the US, I learned the unshakable value of family. This principle has influenced every aspect of my life and career.

Although my mother believed being a physician wasn't the proper lifestyle for a woman, I discovered my passion for medicine. Being a family physician isn't just about diagnosing and treating illnesses. It's about building lifelong relationships, understanding my patients' stories, and supporting them through their joys and challenges. This work aligns with my core values: prioritizing family, nurturing meaningful connections, and ensuring no one feels alone in their healthcare journey.

Yet, as fulfilling as my career was, achieving work-life balance became an intensely personal challenge. I realized how much I had missed during my eldest daughter's first two years while supporting my husband through his medical training in Washington, DC, and working full-time to provide for our family. That deep-rooted guilt over lost moments weighed heavily on me.

When we moved to a different state, we made a conscious decision not to sacrifice but to choose a path that prioritized our family. Through job-sharing and the support of a trusted nanny, I found a way to continue my work as a physician while ensuring our daughters received the love and presence they needed at home. Along the way, I also learned that caring for myself was as important as caring for others. Whether through exercise, reading, or simply taking a breath, I granted myself small but essential "timeouts," which were moments to recharge. My family understood and supported these breaks, knowing I could show up even more fully for them by taking ten minutes of peace for myself.

I've always said I would write a book about my growth, the wisdom I've gained from my personal and professional journey, and the stories of my patients and peers. Motivated by the insights I gained from the Leading Physician Well-being (LPW) certification course offered by the American Academy of Family Practice (AAFP) and my patient experiences, I was compelled to share my journal stories and write this book. The LPW program is a leadership development initiative designed to help physicians address burnout, build resilience, and develop strategies to support their well-being and that of their colleagues. LPW not only taught me skill sets I took back to my team, but I also developed lifelong friendships and support among my team nationally.

I discovered that I am not alone.

I wanted to share my experiences with impostor syndrome (feeling like I'm not my authentic self or enough), the impact of microaggressions, and the lessons I've learned along the way. Writing has always been a therapeutic outlet, allowing me to process and transform my feelings into a narrative that resonates with others. I made a difference in my patients' lives and learned from them that their struggles had antidotes that could be shared with all. I am worthy enough to share what I taught them because it made a difference. I am worthy to continue to learn from them and enrich my role in their caregiving.

Ultimately, the LPW leadership course showed me the importance of sharing my journey from self-doubt to self-empowerment. My team, "Inside Out," gave me the courage to share my story. As I continue to write, I strive to inspire others to embrace their journeys, recognize their worth, and understand that they are not alone in their struggles. The path to self-acceptance and confidence is challenging, transformative, and necessary for personal and professional fulfillment.

This book fulfills that promise. It is my way of sharing the resilience I have developed and offering insight to other doctors, letting them know they are not alone.

I want everyone to pause, take a breath, and reflect on what truly matters to them.

Choose to pursue what brings meaning and joy. Release the expectations others place on you; life is short, and people are important.

Our daily actions should give us a sense of purpose. It is okay to pivot, change perspectives, continue learning and growing, ask for help, and let things go.

Be true to yourself.

You are not alone.

CHAPTER 1

Plot Twist

The ATV lurched, and my stomach dropped. A scream—Was it mine or my daughter's?—cut through the air as we veered off the road. Then, silence fell.

I don't remember the fall. I know now that our ATV hit a bump, and in an instant, we were airborne, plunging twenty-five feet down a cliff.

My brother, riding just behind us, witnessed the entire event. He slammed on his brakes, screaming for help. The others ahead, four family members and our guide, didn't see what happened. But behind us, my husband heard my brother's frantic calls. He turned, saw the empty road where we should have been, and ran toward the edge.

When he looked down, he believed we were both dead.

My daughters' cries cut through the chaos. My brother took control, sending family members back to call emergency services. Then, he and my husband scanned the terrain, looking for a way down. The slope was steep and jagged, with loose rocks and thick brush, but they didn't hesitate.

My husband reached our seventeen-year-old daughter first. She was conscious yet dazed, streaked with blood. Her facial bones and arm were visibly broken. He reassured her and then turned to me.

I lay face down, motionless, my lower left leg twisted, nearly severed. Blood pooled beneath me, my hair dangerously close to the still-spinning ATV wheel. My nephews arrived and stripped off their shirts, pressing them against my wounds to stop the bleeding. My husband knew he had to put emotions aside and go into trauma mode to take control of the situation as a physician. He told my brother-in-law to cradle my leg and keep it stable. My husband directed my brother to help him carefully turn me over, his hands cradling my neck. He braced to see me dead, knowing I had no pulse. He was determined to start CPR.

Then, I took a blood-gurgling shallow breath.

He felt my thready pulse.

Emergency responders arrived, navigating the rugged terrain to reach us. They stabilized my daughter's arm and put her in the first ambulance with my husband. It took eight people to stabilize me and gently get me ten feet down to the road and into the ambulance. Once we reached the hospital in St. Martin, the reality sank in; this facility was ill-equipped for trauma. They stitched my wounds, put a cast on my leg, and placed my daughter's arm in a sling. Her facial fractures would have to wait until we returned home. My leg required urgent surgery, but the first orthopedic surgeon wouldn't arrive for days. The next available medivac was three days away.

The hospital was chaos. Four patients crammed into one room. One convulsing from a seizure. Another was in drug withdrawal. The third had two chest tubes draining blood from a probable gunshot wound. Post-COVID rules allowed only one family member inside. My husband stayed, bouncing between my daughter's bed on the Pediatric wing and mine, exhausted but relentless. He still could not process the situation and continued to be the doctor, flagging down nurses to replace my IV fluids, check my vitals, and assist the patient seizing next to me.

Back at our rental, my other two daughters packed two bags, one for staying and one for leaving. My mother accompanied them, trying to be supportive by being present. She cried and sat on the bed, too shocked to help pack any bags.

My brother refused to accept that we had to wait. He snuck into the hospital, calling every one of his contacts to get us home sooner. He sat by my bed to allow my husband to be with our daughter. My parents and daughters, still at the rental, were overwhelmed with grief and fear. My sisters-in-law uplifted the family, trying to refocus the mood and celebrate New Year's Eve, sending my daughter and me a video of well-wishes for the new year.

By the morning of January 1, my husband made the decision that ultimately saved my life.

He asked the doctor, "If she were your wife, what would you do?"

The answer was immediate. "Get her off the island and back to the US."

That was all he needed to hear. He secured a note stating I was medically stable to fly. I was barely coherent, unaware of the severity of my injuries.

My brother and brother-in-law gathered the family and took them to the airport. My brother pulled my eldest daughter aside. "You have to be strong," he told her, "for yourself, your sisters, and the family. Your dad needs you to take the lead on what he cannot do right now." She pushed aside her grief and pushed herself into check.

My husband carried me from wheelchair to wheelchair, still covered in blood and debris from the day before. My daughters hurried to find anything to support my head, buying a frog travel pillow at the airport gift shop. On the flight home, my husband shook me awake every twenty minutes to ensure I was still alive. He moved my arms and legs to keep my blood circulating.

I was barely conscious.

When we landed in Atlanta for our layover, my husband was ready to call 911. But I stirred, my voice barely above a whisper.

"Just get me home."

That was all he needed to hear.

He called my best friend, who is my job-share partner, to meet us at the Chicago airport. My brother called my cousin for backup. Our friend's husband drove the girls home while my husband and my friend took me straight to St. Mary's Hospital in Madison. The trauma team took over immediately. Within four hours, I was in the OR.

Back home, my parents arrived the next day. My husband took our daughter in for further evaluation. I couldn't remember the accident or why I was in the hospital, so my husband brought me a dry-erase board and wrote down the details to help me piece it together.

You were in an accident. You are in Madison now. We love you.

The recovery was grueling, with surgeries, physical therapy, and the emotional burden of survival. But I wasn't alone. My parents stayed with me for three months. My sister-in-law and her family helped my daughter return to college while her roommates provided support. My husband never left my side. My brother acted when I couldn't. My daughters, shaken by witnessing their mother's near-death experience, leaned on one another. My nephews sacrificed their favorite shirts to stop my bleeding. My sisters-in-law traveled to Madison to care for me, assist me with bathing, and change my dressings. Time, distance, and work responsibilities converged, and the family united.

This was more than an accident.

It was a test of resilience. A testament to family and love. A fight for survival.

I passed the test and won the fight by surviving.

SECTION 1

Self-Reflection and Growth

CHAPTER 2

Wounded Caregiver

The ATV accident happened twenty years after we had moved to Wisconsin, where we prioritized a work-life balance that put family first. I continue to adapt, not just physically but also mentally, to a new normal. My journey back to practicing medicine was characterized by significant changes in my body and my approach to work. The accident left me with several disabilities that were not immediately visible to others but which significantly impacted my daily life.

One of the hardest challenges was a severed cranial nerve (the nerve that controls muscles and sensations in the head and face) that left me unable to move my left eye and caused partial vision loss. I couldn't use one of my eyes, and the prism glasses meant to correct my vision were hard to adjust to, until I finally chose to have surgery to fix my eye in a central position. Even with this correction, turning my head without experiencing disorienting dizziness and double vision was impossible.

Something as simple as looking from side to side, which used to be automatic during patient exams, now required careful and deliberate movements. This changed how I interacted with patients, leading me to rely on technology and voice-command tools like DAX AI (a healthcare industry software that listens to doctors and patients in real-time and generates clinical notes) to handle charting and documentation, as typing had become laborious.

I learned how to read the notes on one screen, which was small enough that my left eye had a full visual of the screen, so I didn't have to track the words. Although I wanted to continue practicing medicine as I had always done, I recognized my new limitations and found ways to adapt. Sitting or standing for extended periods was another hurdle. I rely on an intramedullary pin (metal rod) implanted in my lower leg to stand since the tendons in my knee and ankles are no longer intact.

In the past, I saw a long list of patients, which had me moving quickly from room to room, helping patients onto the exam table, and helping with office emergencies without much thought. Now, sitting for extended periods causes unbearable discomfort. I must be thoughtful of my movements and how I support my frail patients, pace visits carefully, and take moments to sit, stand, or balance myself. Luckily, I realized that one leg was longer than the other and advocated for myself to get orthotics (custom inserts that support and align the feet), which I now cannot live without. I only wear new shoes that accommodate them. With all these changes, I shifted how the clinic operated. Appointments were spaced more thoughtfully, ensuring I had time between patients, which had once felt impossible in the fast-paced medical environment.

There were also days with debilitating headaches, often triggered by staring at the computer screen for too long or by pushing through fatigue. The pain forced me to manage time differently, establishing strict boundaries around work hours. This starkly contrasted with how I used to work, where it was common to stay late to finish paperwork or squeeze in just one more patient. Overworking set me back physically, and honoring those boundaries for my well-being was essential. I still struggle with my super-hero complex, working to honor myself daily.

Another significant change was how I navigated the world outside of work. Something as simple as driving became a challenge, especially in the rain. The movement of the windshield wipers and the rain's disorienting effect on the windows made it impossible to drive safely. As a result, I had to rely on others for transportation, which meant a loss of independence and made it difficult for me to get my daughters to their after-school activities.

Instead of seeing it as a defeat, I embraced a new way of living, focusing on what I could control. With the help of a village of friends, my family found a new version of normal.

Yet, despite all these challenges, none were apparent to my patients. To them, I appeared unchanged, calm, knowledgeable, and compassionate. They asked where I went or if I was retiring, but they didn't notice the double vision, the constant effort to remain standing, or the headaches that followed a long day. I didn't let these unseen obstacles dictate their care but worked around them, finding creative ways to continue providing high-quality care.

For instance, I relied more on verbal cues and meticulously crafted workflows when conducting physical exams. Rather than moving around a patient multiple times, I positioned them strategically to minimize the need to shift and adjust my vision. When I did a skin biopsy or put in an IUD, the patient and instruments were on my right side, a hand's reach away, in an order I knew with my eyes closed. These minor accommodations enabled me to practice medicine with the same level of excellence, even when I had to close my left eye to safeguard my health.

The hardest part was recognizing the need to care for myself just as I cared for my patients. I constantly struggled between the desire to prioritize my patients and the need to protect my well-being. Over time, I realized I couldn't provide my patients with the best care while running on empty. It was no longer about sacrificing everything for the sake of my patients but about finding a balance where both could thrive.

Through all of this, my story became one of resilience and transformation. I adapted to new tools, such as DAX. I changed how I collaborated with my care team. I also accepted that I needed help to function as I once did. These shifts enabled me to practice medicine sustainably for my body and mind. While patients may not have noticed my challenges, those closest to me acknowledged my perseverance.

By embracing these new realities, I could still be the compassionate and skilled doctor I had always been without sacrificing my well-being.

CHAPTER 3

Balancing Acts

The ATV accident wasn't the first life event that allowed me to make accommodations for myself. I spent the first few years of my career working full-time, supporting my family, and striving to meet everyone's needs but my own. Work always came first; it had to. A mortgage, loans, daycare expenses, and daily costs dictated my schedule, and I didn't question it. I barely had time to consider what I wanted. However, I knew I didn't want to miss out on my daughters' lives and the family we wanted to build. Yet, I was missing it, nonetheless. The guilt burned through me during those rare but heavy quiet moments, pressing down on me when I left for work before sunrise and after completing my evening bath and bedtime routines when I returned home.

My family grew, and as a mother, I struggled with the relentless demands of parenting while juggling my professional life. Mornings were a blur of making lunches, checking homework, and rushing out the door, only to spend my workday worrying whether I had been patient or present enough. My children saw me as structured, strict, and even a "tiger mom" who imposed order to navigate the chaos. The pressure to be nurturing and efficient weighed heavily on me each day.

When we moved to a new city, I discovered an opportunity I hadn't thought possible: a job-share as an ambulatory-only provider (a physician who exclusively provides outpatient care). Another physician was in a similar situation, struggling to balance patient care in the hospital and clinic while maintaining what little time she had with her family. We split our panel, managed the in-basket together, and covered for each other when needed. Our patients barely noticed the difference as we built a care team. Sometimes, they even mixed us up, which made us laugh. The care team model lets us be present at work while reclaiming time for ourselves. I started going to the gym. I cooked more meals at home. I spent time with my family without checking my phone or email between bites. For the first time in years, I had space to breathe.

Even with greater balance, I still struggled with something deeper. No matter how hard I tried, I carried the persistent fear that I wasn't good enough.

I had climbed the same ladder as my peers and earned my place in the medical field, yet imposter syndrome clung to me. It whispered that I wasn't as technically skilled, that I was somehow just lucky, and that I didn't belong. I never voiced these thoughts. I assumed that if I admitted my doubts, they would become true. So, I buried them, pushing harder to prove something to myself, my parents, colleagues, and no one in particular.

As a wife, my relationship with my husband often took a backseat to work and parenting. The mental load of balancing our schedules, planning meals, keeping track of school activities, volunteering as managers and leaders, bringing snacks for these activities, and ensuring the house ran smoothly left little room for intimacy. We went weeks without having a real conversation beyond logistics. We needed to reconnect, but finding time for date nights felt impossible. We talked to each other, and through our shared desire for time alone, we discovered that traveling together, even for a short trip, became a way to reconnect with who we were outside of work and parenthood.

Then, one evening after a grueling shift, I chatted with another doctor. We were exhausted, sitting on stiff chairs in our office and engaging in small talk that evolved into something more substantial. Offhandedly, she mentioned that she sometimes felt like a fraud. No matter how many patients she saw or the hours she logged, she couldn't shake the feeling that she wasn't enough. I felt my breath catch; she was articulating my exact experience.

I admitted it to her for the first time as well.

I told her about the doubt that crept in when I hesitated over a diagnosis, the multiple calls to the specialist, and the fear that one day someone would see through me. Instead of judging me, she nodded.

She understood.

In that moment, a weight lifted, and I wasn't alone.

After that, I opened up to more colleagues and was surprised to learn that almost all of them had felt the same way at some point. What started as casual conversations turned into an accidental support network. We began meeting for quarterly dinners where we could talk, vent, and simply be real with each other. Often, we laughed, cried, and offered the kind of support that only fellow providers could understand.

As my clinic grew, that connection evolved into a kind of book club, though my children lovingly called it "wine and whine night," insisting the book was just an excuse to gather. Even now, we still meet. The tradition has endured, just like the friendships it built.

At first, my mentors and peers helped me see what I couldn't. Later, the LPW group and even my own family added their voices to that chorus. The feeling didn't disappear overnight, but its grip gradually loosened. I began to see my worth, not just in my medical expertise but in my ability to connect, solve problems, and truly care.

As a healer, I used to carry the weight of my patients' struggles home with me. The long hours and emotional toll of medicine made it easy to ignore my own needs. I advised patients to prioritize their health, get enough sleep, and ask for help, but I seldom heeded my advice. I gave out my cell number so they could reach out if their health became emergent, but this meant more of my after-clinic time was taken up with my patients. There was a point where I learned that to care for others, I first had to care for myself. That realization didn't come quickly, but it changed everything.

I once thought that balance meant perfection; if I could organize my time effectively, I would finally feel at peace. However, I've learned that balance isn't a destination. It's something I adapt to daily, a constant push and pull between responsibilities, relationships, and self-care. When my accident knocked me off my work-life balance once again, I knew I had to take care of myself first, and then I could sort out the details. I'd done it before, and I could do it again.

Some days, I get it right; others, I don't. Either way, I no longer believe that struggling equates to failing.

I now realize that I'm not alone in this.

CHAPTER 4

Burned, Not Broken

Alyssa had spent over a decade caring for others. Her patients trusted her, her team respected her, and she seemed to have everything under control on the surface. However, behind the closed door of her office, where the weight of the day finally settled, she sensed something slipping away.

Burnout didn't come overnight. It crept in slowly and quietly, like a shadow stretching at the edges of her once-clear purpose. At first, it was exhaustion that coffee couldn't remedy. Then came an unsettling sense of detachment; she was present but not entirely engaged. The work she once loved and the sense of fulfillment she used to experience were replaced by something hollow.

I closed the door behind her as she stepped into my office. Alyssa looked tired, not the kind of tired that sleep could fix but the deep kind that settles into your bones. She sat down quietly, her shoulders tense, her eyes scanning the room before finally landing on mine.

"I don't know if I can keep doing this," she confessed softly.

As her chief, I didn't respond right away. I could tell this wasn't just a hard day. This had been building.

She continued, "I love my patients. I do. But I'm not sure if I love this anymore."

I nodded, letting the silence stretch long enough for her words to settle. I recognized that look. I'd seen it in others, and I'd seen it in the mirror.

"What do you want for yourself?" I asked gently. "Not ten years ago. Now."

She blinked, caught off guard. "I... I don't know."

"If you could redefine your career, what would it include?" I pressed. "And what would you leave behind?"

Alyssa looked down at her hands. "I used to feel so fulfilled. Now I just feel... hollow. Like I'm showing up, but not really there."

I leaned forward. "That's not failure. That's honesty. Most people are too afraid to say it out loud."

She let out a small laugh, but it didn't reach her eyes. "I've spent years telling patients to prioritize their health. I've never given myself the same permission."

We sat with that truth for a moment. Then I said, "Pivoting isn't quitting. It's choosing. And leadership doesn't mean burning out to light the way for others. It means aligning with your purpose, especially when that purpose evolves."

She nodded slowly, the first sign of clarity beginning to return to her face.

I shared insights from my peers' life lessons and the knowledge from my LPW team that had transformed my understanding of burnout and balance. I reminded her that pivoting wasn't quitting, it was a choice. I also reminded her that leadership wasn't solely about guiding others but also aligning oneself with that vision.

We discussed boundaries, reclaiming time, and the radical act of prioritizing one's wellness. Alyssa wasn't walking away from medicine. She was walking toward a version of it that wouldn't cost her everything. She had spent years teaching her patients about self-care yet had never granted herself the same grace. I had been there.

Over time, Alyssa reframed her fears. She stopped viewing change as a loss and began to see it as an evolution. The version of herself that had thrived in the high-demand, high-intensity role wasn't the same person she was today. And that was perfectly fine.

She leaped, not out of desperation but out of intention. In her new role, she immediately felt the difference. She was still a dedicated doctor but no longer running on empty. She felt supported and acknowledged, and for the first time in years, she felt like she belonged, not just in her career but also in her life.

Alyssa's story isn't merely about burnout. It's about permission, the permission to grow, to desire something different, and to redefine what a fulfilling career means.

I drew upon what I had learned from my peers, the LPW course, and my experiences to provide the support I once wished for. I didn't rush to fix things for her. I avoided telling her to push through. Instead, I created space for her to listen to herself. Burnout isn't just about exhaustion, but also disconnection from purpose, joy, and oneself. However, the way back isn't about working harder or proving more. Sometimes, it's about stepping back long enough to ask, What do I need to heal?

Alyssa found her answer. By helping herself, she is now better prepared to assist others in doing the same.

CHAPTER 5

Healing Goes Both Ways

I was the kind of doctor who never put the office out of her mind. Even when I was at home, my thoughts returned to the exam room, hovering over my patients like a silent shadow. I could recall every unfinished chart, uncertain diagnosis, and moments when I might have said something differently or done something better. It didn't matter how many lives I improved; there was always another case, another expectation, and an invisible measure of perfection I failed to meet.

For years, I convinced myself this was the price of being a good doctor. Medicine demanded excellence, and I held myself to an impossibly high standard. If I worked harder, I could outrun my doubts. If I stayed late, took on more responsibilities, and perfected every detail, then maybe, just maybe, I'd feel like I truly belonged in this role.

One afternoon, I met with Mr. Harris, an elderly, longtime patient who battled a chronic illness. He was troubled about not making a lot of progress with his disease.

He entered the exam room with slumped shoulders and eyes filled with frustration. "I don't see the point anymore," he said, rubbing his temples. "I take my medications. I do what I'm told. Yet still, I don't feel like I'm getting anywhere."

His voice was tight with exhaustion, and I recognized it immediately, not only the frustration of a patient in limbo but something more profound: disappointment, self-doubt, and the feeling that no matter how much effort he put in, it would never be sufficient.

I was familiar with that feeling.

I pushed my keyboard aside and turned my body, met his gaze, and said, "Healing takes time, Mr. Harris. You're doing your best, and that's what matters. We all experience setbacks, but that doesn't mean you're failing. It just means you're human."

The words hung in the air between us, laden with truth. Then, there was a shift; I realized I wasn't just speaking to him. I was talking to myself.

How often had I dismissed my efforts because they weren't perfect? How often had I measured my worth by what I hadn't accomplished instead of what I had? I would never tell my patients they were failing because they were struggling, so why did I hold myself to a harsher standard?

That moment cracked something open in me.

Mr. Harris inspired me to embrace self-compassion as a daily practice, not as a vague concept. I spoke to myself as I would to my patients, with understanding rather than criticism and patience instead of punishment.

When impostor syndrome crept in, whispering that I wasn't enough, I reminded myself that even the most seasoned doctors experienced moments of doubt. Just like healing, confidence isn't a linear process. It ebbs and flows, requiring faith that effort, not perfection, is the accurate measure of success.

I made a conscious decision. I adjusted my full-time equivalent (FTE) schedule when I moved to create space for my practice and family. I encouraged my colleagues to do the same, reminding them that being present at home didn't make them any less dedicated as physicians. I spoke openly about burnout, the burdens we carried, and the quiet fear we weren't supposed to acknowledge: What if we weren't as competent as everyone thought?

The more I shared, the clearer the truth became: We were all navigating this together, and just like Mr. Harris, we all deserved grace throughout the process.

I once believed that being a good doctor meant knowing all the answers, making no mistakes, and endlessly sacrificing for my patients. Now, I realize that authentic leadership is different. It involves modeling balance, honesty, and self-respect. It encompasses showing up not just for others but for myself.

Most importantly, I realized perfection is never the objective; being present is.

Maybe that was enough.

CHAPTER 6

Paying It Forward

I learned endurance from my mother. She walks three to five miles a day at nearly eighty, rain or shine. As a child, I didn't appreciate it. In fact, I resented how she seemed to prioritize her workouts over my needs. I didn't understand then that she wasn't walking away from me; she was walking toward herself.

In medical school, exercise became my escape. Between long hours buried in books and the pressure to perform, movement was the only time I could breathe. It gave me space to feel like myself again, but residency made even that difficult. Exhaustion, irritability, fast food, and sleepless nights crept in. I lost touch with my body and myself.

The fundamental shift occurred with my first job. I made a deliberate choice to prioritize my health. It wasn't grand or flashy, just a walk around the neighborhood or a ride on my bike. That's where I rediscovered myself.

I remember calling my mom to say, "Thank you, and I'm sorry." I hadn't realized until then that she'd given me a lifelong gift.

Like many, when COVID hit, I fell into survival mode. Patient needs consumed every hour, and isolation became the norm. Time vanished, and exercise, once a source of strength, was the first thing to go.

One week, feeling completely drained, I realized that something needed to change. I dusted off the elliptical, committing to just twenty minutes daily, and even invested in a Peloton. At first, it felt selfish to take that time when so much needed to be done. But within a week, the change was undeniable. I slept better and felt lighter. That twenty-minute ride evolved into a form of moving meditation, an opportunity to breathe, reflect, and remember who I was.

As I grew physically stronger, my mental clarity returned. The mood swings I had dismissed as inevitable faded away. Calm replaced chaos. I stopped making excuses and viewing self-care as indulgent; instead, it became essential.

Each morning, when I clip onto the bike, it's more than exercise; it's a declaration of self-worth. That feeling of strength and balance rippled through every part of my life: my work, family, and sense of self.

Do I fall off track sometimes? Of course. But I've learned not to spiral when I do. I've learned that even if I pause, I can return. Twenty minutes isn't much in a twenty-four-hour day, but it's enough to return to myself.

Perhaps most importantly, once I had a health routine that worked for me, I could finally recommend self-care to my patients, not as an abstract concept but as something I understood. I had lived the transformation. I still do.

Sarah's Story

Learning to care for myself wasn't just a turning point in my life; it reshaped how I care for others. The more I embraced balance and boundaries, the more I recognized how essential those tools were for my patients. Self-care stopped being a vague suggestion and became a lived truth I could stand behind. One of the first times I truly understood the power of that shift was when I met Sarah.

Sarah had always been the go-to person in her community. Whether organizing church fundraisers, volunteering at her children's school, or managing events for her kids' soccer team, Sarah was always there, smiling, eager to help, and never turning anyone away.

Her calendar was packed with commitments. Mornings began before the sun rose, and nights extended late into exhaustion. She hardly had time to eat, often grabbing fast food from Culver's between errands, soccer practices, and PTA meetings. She convinced herself it was only temporary, that things would slow down eventually. That day never arrived.

By the time Sarah finally came to see me, she was exhausted. She spoke rapidly, enumerating her responsibilities as if she needed to justify them. As she continued, the weariness underlying her words became increasingly undeniable.

"I just need something to help me lose weight," she said, almost pleading. "I don't have time to cook or work out. Perhaps a medication could help?"

I took a moment to consider her request before meeting her gaze. "Sarah, I see how much you do for everyone around you. But if you don't take care of yourself, this pace will eventually catch up with you."

She took a deep breath, preparing for the response she hoped to avoid.

I continued carefully yet firmly. "Weight loss isn't something I can provide in a pill bottle. It's about creating space for yourself. Right now, whether you realize it or not, you're teaching your children that taking care of everyone else is more important than taking care of yourself."

We talked about possible small changes she could start with, and if they made her feel better, to let them grow. "Putting yourself first is not selfish; it is what makes you equipped to tackle everything else."

Sarah's expression changed. She hadn't considered it that way.

As she lay in bed that night, her mind returned to my words. What am I teaching my children? She thought of her daughter, who watched her mother constantly put herself last, and her son, whom she hoped would grow up seeing women as equals, not merely caregivers who drained themselves. Something had to change.

The following evening, Sarah did something that felt unfamiliar. She informed her church group that she could not chair the upcoming fundraiser. She prepared for pushback. Instead, others promptly volunteered to share some of the responsibility. That "no" was a small victory.

Encouraged, Sarah sought more ways to change her habits. Instead of sitting in the stands during her kids' soccer practices, she walked the field. At first, she felt awkward, concerned that other parents would judge her for not sitting with them. However, as she walked, she experienced something she hadn't experienced in a long time: clarity. It wasn't a full workout, but it was movement, and each lap felt like a small triumph. Moms joined her, and connections with others filled her with a joy she had not felt. Walking and talking became a norm.

Gradually, Sarah discovered small ways to reclaim her health. She began preparing simple, nutritious meals, salads with protein, wraps with fresh vegetables, and food that was just as convenient as drive-thru orders, but it left her feeling better. She involved her kids in packing lunches, turning it into a bonding activity that also kept her accountable. The changes weren't drastic or perfect, but they were hers.

Her energy improved, and her clothes fit better. But what surprised her most was how she felt mentally. For the first time in years, she wasn't constantly running on empty, and her family noticed. Her husband took on more evening responsibilities, and her children recognized her efforts and learned from her example.

There were, of course, setbacks. Busy weeks still pulled her into old habits, and the temptation to say "yes" to everything never completely vanished. Each time she hesitated, she reminded herself, This isn't selfish. This is necessary.

As a physician, I've had this conversation many times before. Patients often came to me hoping for a quick fix, a shortcut to undo years of neglecting their health. Frequently, they resisted when I suggested lifestyle changes.

Sarah was no different. Initially, she sought an easy answer. Her willingness to reflect, to embrace discomfort, and to allow it to shift her perspective made her stand out. Each time she returned for a follow-up, I noticed increased confidence and slightly decreased exhaustion. She remained the same Sarah, deeply engaged in her community and committed to her family. The difference was that she also devoted time to herself.

Her journey reinforced my belief that the most effective treatments don't always come in prescriptions. Sometimes, they emerge from conversations.

Sarah's story wasn't merely about weight loss. It was about permitting herself to say no, establishing boundaries, and understanding that taking care of oneself isn't a luxury, it's survival. She imparted this most crucial lesson to her children by prioritizing her needs: Take care of yourself first.

***

Tara's Story

Tara used to feel like she lived two lives, one as an OB/GYN doctor at work and another as a mom at home. Mornings dawned early, racing to the hospital for a before-sunrise delivery, and evenings ended late, charting and folding laundry while trying not to doze off on the couch. Amid managing patient charts, attending soccer games, cooking dinner, and answering late-night calls from the clinic, Tara was always on the move, always balancing, and always stretched thin. The weight of it all felt endless, a quiet pressure behind her ribs that she learned to carry without question.

She was under the same pressure at work, juggling patients, reviewing labs, and managing administrative tasks, which left her breathless. Like many mothers, Tara believed she had to do everything perfectly, that everything would fall apart if she weren't the one holding it all together. I watched her reach a breaking point. I realized that if I didn't tell her she needed to care for herself, she wouldn't have anything left to give to her family or our patients.

I shared with Tara that I was the queen of finding outlets, and it was okay to outsource the things that gave me no joy or that I didn't have time to do well. Her first step was hiring a house cleaner. Initially, it felt like giving up, but she quickly realized how much more energy she had for the things that mattered. Next, she hired someone to take care of the yard work, another task that drained her and her husband's weekends for years. Laundry transformed into a family activity instead of a solo burden. The kids turned it into a game, and suddenly, sorting and folding became a time for laughter and connection.

Tara thanked me for telling her that she didn't need to do it all to be a good mom and doctor. She also trusted my care team's approach to medicine, which included relying on her advanced practitioners and registered nurses and delegating more responsibility to them. Letting go of the need to control everything gifted her with breathing room. She cultivated joy and knew she had peers who understood. Like me, she experienced the relief of letting go.

Learning to take care of myself has benefited my family and patients. It has allowed me to recognize my struggles in others and come alongside them, offering hope and solutions that work. Self-care isn't selfish, as it creates a ripple effect that extends to those within your circle of influence and continues to spread beyond. You never know who you might motivate by prioritizing yourself.

CHAPTER 7

Balancing Medicine and Motherhood

As a family physician, I cherish the deep connections I form with my patients, witnessing them through births, illnesses, and the ups and downs of life. My work was more than a job; it was a calling. I found purpose in supporting others through their challenges, believing medicine and caregiving were inseparable. When my colleague, Jess, delivered her son, Noah, who was born with a rare form of congenital blindness, I watched her world change in ways I never anticipated. I knew she would need more support than our clinic had typically provided.

The diagnosis overwhelmed her. As a physician, Jess understood the science behind congenital conditions, yet no medical training could have prepared her to navigate the healthcare system from the other side. Medical knowledge was both a gift and a burden. She was acutely aware of every possible outcome and every challenge Noah might face.

Research became my colleague's lifeline, and soon, her time was consumed by specialist appointments, therapy schedules, and endless battles with insurance companies. The best care for Noah required a frequent nine-hour car drive to a specialized center in another state.

The dual roles of physician and mother collided daily. Jess's patients required continuity at work, but Noah's medical needs pulled her in another direction. The administrative maze of insurance approvals and referrals left her exhausted. If she, as a physician, struggled with the system, how did parents without a medical background cope? It was a sobering realization.

Jess was more than just a mother at home; she was Noah's advocate, teacher, and guide. Svhe spent hours learning Braille alongside him, exploring tactile learning tools, and connecting with other parents of visually impaired children. She wanted Noah to experience the world fully and understand that his blindness did not limit his possibilities.

Despite her efforts, exhaustion set in. She tried to balance both worlds, but the strain became overwhelming. Guilt weighed heavily on Jess whenever she had to reschedule a patient's appointment or miss an important milestone in Noah's therapy. She loved her work, peers, and patients, but her family had to come first. Realizing that she could not maintain this life left her at a crossroads.

The thought of leaving primary care was heartbreaking. She had spent years building a career she was considering walking away from. The pressure of holding everything together had become too much, and something had to give.

After deep reflection and discussions, Jess explored alternatives. Many physicians were transitioning from traditional practice models to more flexible roles. Urgent care, locum tenens (substitute doctors), direct primary care, and telehealth introduced new possibilities. I don't think she had ever considered practicing medicine outside of a physical clinic, yet telehealth emerged as a solution for her family's needs.

Transitioning to telehealth was not an easy decision. Jess feared losing the in-person connection with her patients and questioned whether it would be as fulfilling. There was also the lingering worry that stepping away from primary care meant she was giving up on her career.

However, as she adapted to this new role, we all learned that working in telehealth medicine allowed for comprehensive and diverse patient care. Jess discovered something unexpected: She could still build meaningful patient relationships. She learned how to connect through a screen and listen in ways that transcended physical presence. Many patients appreciated the accessibility, and she found a renewed purpose in providing care that fit into their lives and hers.

For the first time in years, Jess's life was balanced. She no longer had to choose between being a good physician and a present mother. Telehealth enabled her to arrange work around Noah's therapies and be there for him without compromising her career. The weight that had burdened her for so long was lifting.

Her guilt about changing career paths faded as Jess learned that flexibility is not a sign of failure but a reflection of resilience. Success wasn't about pushing through exhaustion at all costs; it was about adapting and finding new ways to honor her passion for medicine while caring for her family.

Through this experience, Jess's empathy for her patients deepened. She viewed work through a new lens, recognizing the countless individuals navigating their challenges, parents balancing work and caregiving, patients advocating for their health, and families making tough choices. There was no single "right" way to be a doctor, just as there was no one way to define success.

The evolution of Jess's career mirrors a broader shift in medicine. More physicians are rethinking the traditional demands of the profession, seeking ways to practice without sacrificing their well-being. Direct primary care, shift-based work, and telemedicine are not signs of doctors "stepping away" but of adaptation to the realities of modern life.

Jess no longer needs to prove she can do it all, and Noah's journey is still unfolding. She learned that choosing a sustainable path did not mean sacrificing her identity as a physician. Instead, it means embracing a new version of herself that allows her to be a doctor, mother, caregiver, and an individual all at once.

This story isn't unique. It echoes the experiences of many physicians striving to align their lives with what matters most. True success lies not in how much we endure, but in how well we find that balance.

CHAPTER 8

Fake Smiles

For years, I cultivated the art of the fake smile, wearing it like a badge of honor. It projected confidence and warmth to everyone around me, staff, patients, and peers who marveled at my apparent ease. Little did they know that beneath that cheerful facade churned a tumultuous sea of emotions, a powerful tide of stress, grief, and overwhelming vulnerability that threatened to pull me under at any moment. This duality, the beautiful illusion I created, was my unspoken struggle, my hidden story waiting to be told.

Every day began with the ritual of putting on that smile, knowing that as a doctor, my role demanded an unwavering facade. The loss of a beloved family member had created a void that echoed in every corner of my life. Yet, the world outside did not pause for grief, my patients' grief or mine. Patients needed care, families sought comfort, and colleagues looked to me for leadership.

As I moved from room to room, my smile remained firmly in place, but the weight of unexpressed emotions grew heavier. In one room, a patient named Clara struggled with grief after losing her father. I listened intently, offering words of empathy while feeling the sting of loss seep into the conversation. I connected deeply to Clara's pain, yet I kept my smile and emotions intact even as I empathized, concealing the storm brewing within.

Just down the hall, I entered another room where a new mom sat with her joyful baby. The stark contrast was palpable. While the baby cooed and giggled, the mother's eyes were filled with sadness and exhaustion from the realities of postpartum depression. I offered words of encouragement, trying to lift her spirits, all the while feeling the weight of their unaddressed grief. I understood how important it was to be present for the mother, but inside, I felt a pang of sorrow for her struggles, wishing I could share my vulnerabilities.

Next, a joyful visit to an elderly patient, Mr. Thompson, who was celebrating his eightieth birthday. The room was filled with balloons and laughter, and as I entered, his smile widened; however, underneath my smile was a bittersweet ache. I reflected on how fleeting life is and how the reality of loss often overshadows moments like these. I celebrated with Mr. Thompson, but each cheer felt like a tug at my heart, awakening the pain of my recent loss.

Then, I entered the next room, where a younger patient, Ella, anxiously awaited her test results. The news was grim: breast cancer. The smile felt like a mask slipping away as I delivered the diagnosis. At that moment, the weight of the world was unbearable. I had to embody strength and compassion for Ella, but my heart ached for her impending journey and the fear surrounding her.

As we spoke, it took every ounce of energy to maintain a plastered smile and be a beacon of hope while, inside, I was struggling with heavy emotions of fear, sorrow, and compassion. Observing her deceivingly young, healthy body juxtaposed with the stark reality of what the cancer was doing inside it seemed impossible to accept.

I navigate moments like these daily, shifting from a Medicare patient needing chronic care to a well-woman exam and then back to another complex visit, twenty-plus appointments a day. I smile, stay composed, and remain fully present, empathetic, and supportive through each emotional turn.

The facade felt like a performance, with each room transforming into a stage for the emotional turmoil I was determined to conceal. I left my true feelings at the door, navigating through laughter, tears, and heartache, wearing a smile as a shield. With every interaction, the weight of unexpressed grief and stress only grew heavier.

Finally, at the end of the day, when the office was quiet and the lights dimmed, I found a moment of solitude. The fake stoic smile slipped away in that stillness, revealing the exhaustion and heartache I had tucked away. The walls that dammed my pain suffocated me, so I let the tears flow freely. It was a release, a reminder that an empathetic human being lay within, beneath my white coat and ever-present smile.

In those moments of vulnerability, I realized that while being a doctor required a specific strength, it was also essential to honor my emotions. I recognized the need to seek support and find spaces to safely express the grief, stress, and complexity of my experiences. No one should have to bear such a heavy burden alone, and it was time to acknowledge that even the strongest caregivers need moments to grieve, feel, and heal. The journey ahead required balance, finding ways to care for myself as intensely as I cared for my patients.

It was okay to feel and express joy or hardship with them.

We are all in this together.

CHAPTER 9

Lessons in Patience, Presence, and Letting Go

Structure and precision have always been my anchors. As a doctor, these traits serve me well. No detail goes overlooked; every patient's treatment plan is meticulously tailored, and high standards guide my work. Perfectionism seems like a strength in medicine, yet outside the clinic, it has influenced my home life in ways I never fully understood. I held my family to those same impossible standards for years, expecting order, efficiency, and control over life's unpredictable nature. I realized that my need for structure often conflicted with the reality of human relationships.

My first lesson was with my ten-year-old daughter, Mia. She brims with creativity, curiosity, and spontaneity. While I thrive in structure, she finds joy in unplanned moments.

One night, she stood before me in tears, overwhelmed by an unfinished school project that had been due for weeks.

My frustration surfaced immediately. "Mia, why didn't you start earlier? You had ample time!" My voice was sharper than I intended, and her face crumpled beneath its weight.

Her response was quiet, but it cut deep. "Mom, I'm just not like you. I am not perfect and never will be."

Those words carried a truth I had long ignored. My expectations for her reflected my own, relentless, strict, and often unfair. She was not a miniature version of me; she was her own person, navigating the world in a way that made sense to her.

That night, an apology replaced my lecture. "I'm sorry, Mia. I don't need you to be like me. I want you to be you."

Instead of dictating how to finish her project, I allowed her to take the lead. She worked in her own way and at her own pace, completing it with a sense of accomplishment. Initially, letting go of my need to control the process felt unnatural, yet I learned to trust her instincts. I still practice taking a step back from my immediate response to inhale and let Mia vent, view, and revise her path. I love her for being herself, and I must remind myself that it cannot be my path; sometimes, she doesn't need my unsolicited advice. When I take a breath and pause, I create space for patience.

Another revelation came from my husband, Adam. His approach to life is the opposite of mine, unhurried and open to spontaneity and finding joy in detours. One Saturday, I meticulously planned a family outing, organizing every activity down to the hour. Excited to execute my perfect itinerary, I presented the schedule over breakfast.

Adam simply smiled. "Let's just see where the day takes us."

The suggestion annoyed me. Thoughtful planning guarantees the best experiences, right?

The day unfolded differently than I expected. A last-minute decision led us to a quiet picnic in a park we had never visited. A spontaneous stop at a street fair immersed us in live music and local cuisine. Old friends crossed our paths, transforming a simple outing into an evening filled with shared laughter and joy. By nightfall, it was clear that no itinerary could have orchestrated a better day.

Adam nudged me playfully. "See? Not so bad to go with the flow."

He was right. The need to control every moment distracted me from the joy of just being present. Breathe and Let Go.

The most challenging lesson I learned came from my parents. They raised me with discipline and high expectations, always expressing pride in my accomplishments while also worrying about the toll my career took on my well-being.

One holiday, after a long and grueling week on call, I arrived at their home feeling exhausted. My mother greeted me with concern, her voice tinged with something heavier. "You know, family matters, too."

The words stung. A quiet guilt settled in, though I quickly masked it with reassurances. "I'm fine, Mom. Work has just kept me busy." The words felt hollow even as I spoke them.

Later that night, as we gathered around the dinner table, I allowed myself to be honest for the first time in years. "I don't always have it together. I try, but it's difficult." My voice trembled under the weight of that admission.

Across the table, my mother softened in a way I had never noticed before. In that moment, I realized that vulnerability did not make me weak; it allowed me to be fully seen.

These lessons extended beyond my home. They changed the way I interacted with my patients.

Mrs. Jenkins, one of my longtime patients, often filled our visits with stories about her life, repeating details I had heard before. Previously, I listened while watching the clock, silently calculating how far behind schedule I was. Everything changed after I learned to embrace patience.

During one visit, I released my need to keep things moving. I listened, not just as a doctor but as someone who recognized the importance of being heard.

When she finished, she took my hand. "Thank you for listening. You have no idea how much that means to me." Breathe and Be Present.

Through my family, I discovered a strength that went beyond discipline. True resilience doesn't depend on rigid control but flexibility, patience, and presence. The lessons were challenging, especially when they didn't align with my innate personality, but they were exactly what I needed. Releasing my impossible expectations didn't make me any less of a doctor, wife, or mother; it made me more.

As I move forward, I carry these truths with me, aware that they have transformed me in ways that no medical training ever could. The aim is connection, not perfection. The deepest growth comes not from mastering others but from understanding myself.

SECTION 2

Personal Experiences and Challenges

CHAPTER 10

DEI Microaggressions

The day I was accepted into medical school, I felt the weight of my father's dreams and my mother's concerns settle on my shoulders. As the daughter of immigrants, their sacrifices and silent aspirations shaped my journey. It was never just about my goal of becoming a doctor; it was my unspoken promise to honor the struggles they endured. This moment wasn't just a personal victory but a testament to the hope they instilled in me. It was proof that their hard work had not been in vain.

I worked tirelessly, surviving the demanding training regimen and striving for excellence. The expectations were high, but I rose to them. Even after residency, after years of demonstrating my abilities in every way possible, there was still a lingering question: Was I good enough?

Despite my credentials, knowledge, and the long nights I spent mastering my craft, a quiet but persistent fear followed me. It whispered during moments of exhaustion, in brief interactions with colleagues, and in the subtle hesitations I noticed from others when I spoke.

I often found myself in rooms where I was the only woman of color, the only one without a family legacy in medicine, and the only one who had to translate my parents' documents while preparing for exams. Many of my colleagues had inherited their place in this profession, growing up in households where medicine was a given, not a hard-fought battle. I had earned my seat at the table, yet I still felt like an outsider. Microaggressions only reinforced that feeling.

A senior physician once glanced at my badge and asked, "Where did you train again?" The emphasis lingered, heavy with skepticism. Patients sometimes mistook me for a nurse or an assistant, even as I stood in my white coat with my stethoscope draped around my neck.

Compliments often carried underlying assumptions.

"You're so articulate."

"Your English is perfect!"

"You must have worked twice as hard to get here."

I had worked twice as hard. Yet, hearing it spoken aloud and framed as a compliment made me feel even more like an outsider. No matter how many hours I put in or how many lives I touched, there was always a subtle suggestion that I needed to prove myself just a little more.

One evening, after a tough shift, when self-doubt pressed harder than usual, I stood in front of a mirror. The exhaustion was evident: dark circles under my eyes and shoulders weighed down by another day spent struggling to belong. A thought surfaced, one I had never allowed myself to acknowledge fully. What if the problem isn't me? What if my feelings of inadequacy weren't a reflection of my actual ability but rather a byproduct of a system that had made me believe I needed to prove my worth repeatedly?

I reflected on my journey, the sacrifices, the late nights, the patients who had thanked me, and the moments when my hands had brought healing. No amount of luck had brought me here. I had earned every step of this path.

I made a decision.

I would no longer allow imposter syndrome to dictate my sense of belonging. The internalized doubt, the constant comparison, and measuring my worth against the expectations of others would stop with me.

Each day, I rewrote the narrative. I reminded myself that I was more than enough, that I had not just made it in medicine, I had thrived and excelled in it. My voice mattered. My presence mattered. I had just as much right to be in this profession as anyone else.

Over time, I shared my experiences. Young doctors, nurse practitioners, and physician assistants, especially those from backgrounds like mine, confided in me about their struggles with self-doubt. I saw the same insecurities reflected in their eyes, the same fear of being perceived as outsiders, and the same quiet exhaustion from carrying more than just their dreams.

"I feel like I don't belong," one medical student confided.

I met her gaze, steady and sure. "You do. You belong here just as much as anyone else." The words weren't merely for her but also for me.

Imposter syndrome once made me question my place in this field, but that's no longer true.

I earned my way here and refuse to diminish my success by doubting it.

I am not just a doctor but a living testament to resilience, hard work, and the power of breaking barriers.

I belong.

CHAPTER 11

The Quiet Revolution

Katrina had always been passionate about engineering, a field where she believed she could make a meaningful difference. However, as a Hispanic woman in a predominantly male and primarily white conservative community, she frequently faced subtle yet persistent microaggressions. Colleagues dismissed her ideas in meetings, assuming she was merely support staff rather than an engineer. Comments like "You're pretty smart for a girl" left her feeling marginalized and undervalued.

After a tiring week, Katrina visited my office for a routine check-up. Frustration and sadness overwhelmed her. When I entered the exam room, I immediately noticed Katrina's unusual demeanor.

As I looked at Katrina, I felt a twinge of concern. "Hi, Katrina! How have you been feeling?" I asked, hoping my voice didn't betray my deep worry. It was always hard to see her this way, and I knew how much she struggled beneath her brave facade.

Katrina took a deep breath, feeling the weight of her experiences. "Honestly, I've been struggling. Being a woman in engineering is challenging, and I often feel like I'm constantly encountering microaggressions. It's draining."

I nodded empathetically. "I can only imagine how that feels. It's essential to discuss these experiences and not keep them bottled up. How have you been coping?"

Katrina expressed her frustrations about her job, her father's worries about the conflict in Israel, and her brother's challenges with being transgender and living with HIV. Each topic added another layer of stress to her already complicated life. "It's just so much to handle, and I feel like I can't escape it," she admitted, her voice trembling.

I listened closely, then replied, "It sounds like you're carrying a heavy burden. It's important to have a support system. Have you thought about reaching out to a therapist who specializes in microaggressions and identity issues? They can assist you in processing these feelings and developing coping strategies."

Katrina had never considered that. "I didn't know that was an option," she replied, hopefully.

"Also, let's discuss practical daily strategies," I continued. "For example, when someone makes a microaggressive comment, respond assertively. You might say, 'I appreciate your perspective, but I'd like to clarify that my abilities are not tied to my gender.' It's essential to reclaim your narrative and assert your presence."

As our conversation progressed, I helped Katrina explore ways to build her confidence. We discussed the significance of surrounding herself with supportive peers and mentors who could validate her experiences. I also encouraged Katrina to join a women-in-engineering group to connect with others who understood her challenges.

"Remember, Katrina, you're not alone in this," I assured her. "Your feelings are valid, and seeking support when needed is okay."

With newfound determination, Katrina left the appointment feeling empowered. She scheduled a session with a therapist and practiced the assertive responses I had suggested. Over time, Katrina learned to navigate her workplace challenges with greater confidence. She engaged in open discussions about diversity and inclusion, gradually changing the dynamics of her team.

Katrina also took a proactive approach to support her brother. She encouraged him to connect with local LGBTQ+ organizations, helping him build a supportive network while navigating the challenges of being a transgender person in a conservative community. They found comfort in sharing their experiences, realizing their journeys were intertwined.

Katrina learned she didn't have to endure microaggressions in silence; she could use her voice and experiences to foster understanding and acceptance. Every step she took for herself and her brother helped her reclaim her identity and empower others in her community.

Katrina emerged as a resilient engineer and a champion for change, paving the way for future generations of women and minorities in her field. She recognized that while the journey was challenging, it was rich with opportunities for growth and connection. Whenever needed, I remained a constant source of support, guiding her through life's complexities with compassion and wisdom.

CHAPTER 12

Get Up and Walk Out

It was a typical Saturday morning clinic, a special service we offered to help patients who couldn't take time off work for their preventive or routine health care needs. Saturdays were always busy, with strict policies in place, especially regarding narcotic refills, which we only managed if we were the patient's primary care provider (PCP). This rule aimed to ensure the safe and consistent management of controlled substances, yet occasionally, someone would attempt to bypass it.

I was prepared for the day's appointments when a patient I hadn't seen before, a polite-looking woman in her forties, walked in. Her chart showed she had an appointment for an annual exam, but she insisted she was there for a medication refill. As I reviewed her history, I noted she was overdue for a pap smear and a mammogram, so I decided to take a comprehensive approach and address her overall health needs during our time together.

We began with a discussion of her chronic conditions, hypertension, weight management, and preventive screenings. I encouraged her to stay active and reviewed her diet, contraception, blood pressure control, and upcoming colon and breast cancer screenings. It was a thorough, productive visit, until, almost as an afterthought, she mentioned she was there to refill her oxycodone.

When I looked further into her chart, I saw she hadn't seen her PCP in nearly two years and had been receiving sporadic narcotic refills from multiple providers across the state, most through urgent care visits. I kindly but firmly explained that we had a policy in place: Only her established PCP, with whom she had a narcotic agreement, could refill her controlled medications. I also mentioned I would order a urine drug screen, per safety protocol.

That's when everything shifted. Her tone became combative. She insisted the only reason she had made this appointment was to get her narcotics. I calmly reiterated that she had been scheduled for an annual visit, not a narcotic refill, and that our clinic couldn't make exceptions to the policy.

Her frustration boiled over. She stood up, pointed at me, and shouted, "This is why I don't see foreign doctors!"

Her words hit like a slap. For a moment, I was stunned. I am as American as you are, I thought. Born and raised here. My nationality has no bearing on the policies that protect patient safety or my qualifications as a physician. But I held my breath, steadied myself, and refused to let her rattle me.

"I believe our appointment is over," I said calmly. "I won't charge you for today's visit. I'll leave your wellness orders in the system, but you'll need to follow up with your primary care provider for your refills."

She looked stunned, caught off guard that I had stood my ground. She wasn't used to being told no, especially not by someone who looked like me. Then, frustration returned to her face as she demanded that I finish the exam.

I repeated myself firmly, "This appointment is complete. There will be no further examination or prescriptions today."

I left the room, and she followed me out into the hallway, insisting that she had paid a copay and demanding her oxycodone. Once again, I stated that the appointment had been terminated, she would not be charged, and she would need to follow up with her PCP. She had to be escorted from the clinic by security and yelled behind her that she would report me to my boss.

I told her, "You're welcome to contact patient relations if you'd like, but our appointment is over."

Then I called my clinic manager to document the encounter. I knew a patient complaint would likely follow. The incident had cost me over thirty minutes and caused delays for my remaining patients, many of whom had witnessed part of the commotion. But I had done the right thing. I had upheld clinic policy, maintained patient safety, and stood firm against a personal attack.

That experience reminded me that my role as a physician extends beyond clinical care to encompass a broader range of responsibilities. Sometimes it means asserting boundaries, protecting the integrity of medical practice, and refusing to be diminished by someone's prejudice. I was proud of my heritage and my profession. No insult, no matter how personal, would change that.

CHAPTER 13

To Trellis or Not to Trellis

For over two decades, a simple trellis stood watch in my backyard, a lovely structure that framed the garden, adding a touch of privacy to our little haven. However, storms had come and gone, and recent weather upheavals had taken their toll. Once proud and upright, the trellis now leaned precariously as if caught in a sway between standing strong and surrendering to gravity. As my children dashed around, their laughter piercing the air, a knot of worry twisted in my stomach. I envisioned the trellis collapsing, a wooden giant toppling into their world of playful innocence. Seeking a solution, I reached out to my neighbors, hoping to find a carpenter who could breathe new life into the fixture. When I finally called someone they recommended, his friendly voice offered reassurance. He quoted twenty dollars an hour plus supplies, estimating the job would take only two days. I found myself nodding along, even as my instinct whispered caution. When I asked about a contract, he waved it off with a confident laugh, claiming his work spoke for itself. Trust, I realized, was often a leap into the unknown, and in that moment, I took the plunge, buoyed by his reputation and the shared stories of trusted neighbors.

On the second day, I took my daughters out to see the dismantled trellis and the piles of wood and lattice cluttering our patio. I was eager for them to steer clear of the construction area and made sure they stayed at a safe distance. As we chatted, I learned more about the carpenter's life and work, even bringing him lemonade and cookies to make him feel welcome. Eventually, he asked about my job, and I shared that I was a part-time physician, balancing my profession with raising my three children. He seemed to focus on my being a doctor, his tone shifting as he inquired about which clinic I worked at. He was familiar with the clinic because his provider was my partner. He started asking medical questions and wanted my advice on his wife's dementia and diabetes concerns. I politely explained that I didn't discuss health issues outside the clinic, especially in front of my children, and emphasized that I wanted to focus on being a mom when I was at home.

By the fourth day, I was surprised to see only one post installed. He became defensive when I asked him about the timeline, reminding him of the initial two-day estimate. The hours had added up, and we had reached $640, plus an additional $200 for materials. He claimed it would "take as long as it needed" and insisted that, as a doctor, I should have no trouble affording his services. Shocked, I tried to remain calm, explaining that I needed a written contract to proceed. I suggested that he leave for the day until he could provide one, leaving the project as is.

This only seemed to infuriate him further. His face flushed, he began yelling, throwing his equipment around, and accusing me of being a "bad doctor." He even suggested that if he had a heart attack, I would be responsible. I calmly told him I would call 911 if he needed emergency assistance, but I couldn't treat him on my property. Still, he continued his outburst until I had no choice but to call the police to remove him from my premises. Before he left, I handed him a check for $1,200, considering the job done, as I could no longer work with him.

In the days that followed, the situation escalated. The carpenter repeatedly called my clinic, left messages with patient relations, and even contacted the legal department, trying to file complaints to have me fired. When they informed him that this was not a medical issue and suggested he seek legal counsel, I hoped that would be the end.

But then, one morning, he showed up at my front door. His eyes were filled with anger as he warned me he was determined to "ruin" me and my career. His words cut deeper when he added that, as a "brown woman," I had "no rights in America" and that he would demonstrate just how powerless I was. A wave of fear rolled through me, but I managed to stay composed long enough to call the police again. I immediately filed a restraining order, hoping this would finally put an end to the harassment. A sympathetic officer even offered to help with the trellis, joking that he and his friends could set it up for half the price. I thanked him, laughing despite the stress, and assured him I'd figure something out.

Months passed as I tried to move on from the ordeal. Then, a letter arrived from the medical board stating that a complaint had been filed against my license, alleging I had "refused care." The accusation felt surreal. My legal team reassured me there was no merit to the case. Still, the investigation dragged on for three months, forcing me to repeatedly recount every detail of the incident, gather evidence, and wait anxiously for the board's decision. Ultimately, the case was dismissed, but the experience left me shaken.

After the ordeal, I spoke with my partner, who had decided to continue seeing the carpenter as a patient. While I respected his decision, I requested that my team and I not be involved in his care to maintain boundaries. It was a relief to know I wouldn't have to interact with him in any capacity in the future.

Reflecting on the experience, I learned the importance of always having a written contract, regardless of how "trustworthy" a person may appear. I also realized that revealing my profession could make me a target for those who believe that being a doctor equates to having unlimited financial resources. Most painful of all, I was reminded that my ethnicity and gender could still be weaponized against me in the eyes of some. Throughout it all, I had remained calm, followed the proper steps, and reassured myself that doing the right thing would ultimately protect me.

Patient Interactions and Compassionate Care

CHAPTER 14

Mirror, Mirror on the Wall, Who Am I Kidding?

Standing in front of the mirror, I often struggled to see my true self reflected. The image that faced me felt like a mask, a facade molded by expectations and pressures. As a physician, I had learned to appreciate the complexities of my patients, yet I found it difficult to extend that same compassion to myself. This internal conflict was heightened when I encountered a patient who exemplified resilience, devotion, and strength despite her challenges.

Diana, a cherished patient, comes to mind when I think about inner spirits. Hers shone brighter than any physical challenge she faced. Although her journey with weight had been tumultuous, what struck me most was her unwavering devotion to God and her profound spiritual self. Every conversation we shared brimmed with a sense of faith that transcended her struggles. Yet, like me, she often found it hard to recognize the incredible person within her.

As we discussed her challenges, it became clear that she was burdened by the weight of societal expectations, both for herself and for others. She often equated her worth with her appearance, leading to a cycle of frustration, self-doubt, and overwhelming disappointment with herself. I empathized with her; I knew what it felt like to be trapped in a narrative that valued outward appearances over inner strength.

Determined to help her change this perspective, I devised a small but meaningful exercise. I asked her to take three wooden crosses and place each one in a small black box, wrapping each in different paper wrappings. The first was to be covered in shimmering gold sparkle paper, the second in holiday-themed wrapping paper, and the last in an old newspaper or a brown paper bag. Each paper symbolized different layers of perception, how we often judge value by outward appearances. I instructed her to set each of the boxes on her mantel, and when self-doubt crept in, she could go to the mantel and see that inside, they were all the same and equally spiritually devoted. The outward appearance did not matter.

I had to remind her many times that, although the outside of each cross looked different, the true essence of the cross remained the same. It represented her intrinsic worth, one that societal standards could not diminish. I encouraged her to place these crosses on her mantel as a daily reminder that beauty and value come from within, not from the judgments of the outside world.

As the months passed, I observed a change in her. She opened up both to me and her therapist about her binge eating, which she had kept hidden for years. She discussed her self-expectations, which she felt were predetermined by her ancestors. During each visit, she spoke not only about her physical health but also about her emotional and spiritual growth. The crosses became more than just visual reminders; they inspired careful reflections on self-worth. She saw herself from a new perspective, highlighting her strengths, faith, and self-love.

This shift enabled her to release the stress of conforming to external ideals. She began prioritizing self-care, not only in terms of diet and exercise, but also in nurturing her spiritual life and emotional well-being. The weight of societal pressures diminished, creating room for a healthier mindset.

Over time, her physical health also improved. She approached weight management with a newfound sense of empowerment, rather than shame. By addressing her emotional and spiritual needs, she discovered a holistic approach to wellness that transformed her life. Her laughter became more authentic, and her faith deepened, reflecting a woman who had come to embrace all facets of herself.

In our final session, she shared how those wooden crosses had transformed her life. She had always had a strong predisposition for faith and God. She found the strength to start a ministry. Standing in front of the mirror, she finally saw a reflection that embodied resilience, strength, and faith. The journey had been about so much more than weight; it was about embracing her true self, inside and out.

I realized that I, too, was on a similar journey. Her transformation inspired me to reflect on my struggles with self-acceptance. If she could learn to see herself through the lens of love and spirituality, perhaps I could also. It served as a powerful reminder that we are worthy and we benefit from recognizing our inner beauty.

Our shared experiences taught me that the road to self-acceptance is not a solitary journey. Together, we discovered the importance of looking beyond outward appearances and embracing each other's unique essence.

While helping her find her true self and rereading my journals, I, too, discovered aspects of myself, reminding me that we are all beautifully complex individuals worthy of love and respect, just as we are.

CHAPTER 15

On Her Terms

Gretchen's cancer journey was emotional and marked with resilience, and I carry it with me still. I had seen Gretchen for years as a patient and a medical translator. When she was in her late fifties, her heartburn symptoms increased, so I treated her with Prilosec to decrease gastric reflux. The treatment didn't help, and Gretchen pushed past her symptoms as they worsened.

About three months later, during a visit, I noticed how pale her skin was and that she had lost weight. I advised her to schedule an appointment with me to use a scope to examine her stomach. Although I placed the order for the procedure that day, she did not schedule it until three months later or make a follow-up appointment. I saw her in the office halls and encouraged her to make the GI appointment. She responded that she was doing okay.

When Gretchen finally had the scan completed, we found a large mass.

She was diagnosed with gastric cancer, and she declined conventional Western treatments, opting instead for alternative remedies. This decision reflected her desire to take control of her life, and she visited my office only when she was strong enough or when her symptoms overwhelmed her. Gretchen also saw me to discuss how her family was handling her choice. Her experience was not just about facing illness; it was about her effort to navigate a challenging world, leaving a lasting impression on everyone she encountered.

Gretchen's family struggled to accept her decision. They wanted her to receive every possible medical treatment, hoping to extend her life. An undercurrent of tension and grief marked their visits as they struggled to respect her wishes while fearing they were watching her slip away without doing enough. Conflict hung in the air during every appointment; a poignant reminder of the burden her decision would place on those who loved her most. Despite their differences, they eventually understood her perspective, which was rooted in independence and dignity. The acceptance didn't make it any easier.

In the following months, I provided Gretchen with as much support and care as she allowed. We talked extensively about managing her symptoms, considering dietary adjustments, herbal supplements, and other natural treatments to alleviate her pain. She inquired about IV fluids to help maintain her hydration during her most challenging days, and we discussed simple adjustments she could implement to prevent further weakening of her body. I listened without pressure or judgment as she navigated her unique path toward peace.

As her condition worsened, Gretchen sensed she was nearing the end of her journey and asked me to help arrange for hospice care in her home. Her family struggled with this decision, unsure if they could be strong enough to honor her wishes to pass away peacefully without the interventions they had once begged her to try. However, over time, they understood her vision for her final days and ultimately found comfort in allowing her to go on her terms, surrounded by those she loved.

In Gretchen's final weeks, I received a heartfelt letter from her. She expressed gratitude for the support, our conversations, and for respecting her decisions throughout her illness. Soon after her passing, her family sent a letter thanking me for honoring their mother's wishes and helping them find the courage to support her in ways that challenged their instincts. They conveyed their appreciation for the gentle care, the pain management options, and the time at home that allowed them to say goodbye in a manner that felt true to her.

Their letters emphasized the significance of honoring each patient's journey, especially when it involves difficult, soul-searching choices. As family medicine doctors, we are called not only to treat illnesses but also to accompany our patients through every aspect of their journey, wherever it may lead. This experience reminded me of the importance of respecting a patient's choices while supporting families in honoring their loved one's path.

This experience taught me that respect and empathy are fundamental to patient-centered care. Witnessing my patient's family struggle but ultimately support her in the face of terminal illness revealed the resilience and complexity everyone brings to their healthcare experiences. I learned that even when a patient's choices diverge from medical norms or family expectations, they can still be honored in ways that uphold the patient's dignity and autonomy.

Navigating the tension between Gretchen's desires and her family's concerns deepened my knowledge of the delicate balance we must maintain as providers. I learned that sometimes, our role is less about steering patients toward a specific decision and more about creating a safe space where they are empowered to make choices that align with their values. By listening without judgment, I gained a deeper understanding of Gretchen's perspective and provided care that she accepted on her terms. This lesson in humility, learning to step back and honor what felt right for her, reshaped my approach to patient care.

I also recognized the importance of supporting families through the emotional and moral complexities they face when dealing with terminal illnesses. By involving her family in every step of the process, I offered them a way to share in her final chapter that honored her spirit and legacy. In the end, they, too, found peace in the choice to allow her to pass with grace and autonomy, and their gratitude reminded me that our care extends to the loved ones who carry on the legacy of our patients. This experience underscored that family medicine entails treating the whole person and supporting their families, particularly during life's most challenging moments.

CHAPTER 16

Echoes of Clara

One of the most defining moments in my career as a family medicine doctor emerged from the care of a remarkable woman named Clara, who was only forty-two when she succumbed to metastatic breast cancer. Reflecting on her case, I realize it was unique in countless ways, each imparting profound lessons about the essence of patient care, insights that continue to shape my practice and approach to healing today.

Clara came to me with persistent hip pain that had plagued her for several months. She had seen our physician's assistants twice, been to nine physical therapy appointments, and visited the massage therapist to no avail. She had continued her preventive care needs and had undergone her routine mammogram three months before seeing me, and all the results were clear, no signs of cancer, no red flags. However, when I met her in the clinic, my instincts kicked in; the duration and severity of her pain raised questions that my training hadn't prepared me to confront.

I suggested a hip X-ray, driven by an intuition that something was off. What we uncovered shattered expectations: a lesion. I immediately arranged for her to see an orthopedic surgeon for a biopsy. Two weeks later, when she returned for the results, the lesion in the hip quietly revealed itself to be metastatic from breast cancer. That moment marked the beginning of an unforgettable journey for Clara and me, highlighting the fragile balance between hope and despair, the power of intuition in medicine, and the deep connections we forge with our patients. Her story remains a vivid chapter in my ongoing quest to provide thoughtful and compassionate care.

The path forward was filled with difficult conversations and profound human connections. I sat with Clara's husband and family to share the devastating news. Together, we navigated the rollercoaster of her treatments, but her body continued to weaken. Clara chose to receive IV fluids in our clinic after her chemotherapy sessions, feeling more at home there. During those visits, we discussed her little joys, her time with her children, and the moments of happiness she still found despite her struggles.

I wasn't directly treating the breast cancer; her oncologist handled that, but I realized I was addressing something far more significant: I was caring for her spirit, her comfort, and her family's well-being. Over the next six months, she bravely fought, but ultimately, the disease prevailed. After her passing, her husband came to see me, and through tears, thanked me for being there, for providing more than just medical care, and for offering comfort to his wife and their family during a time of unimaginable pain.

This experience taught me that family medicine is more than diagnoses, medications, and treatments. It involves seeing the person behind the disease, standing with families during their most challenging moments, and fostering a sense of peace and connection when the outcome is beyond our control. I carry her story with me as a reminder that medicine is about curing and caring.

One of the most rewarding aspects of being a physician is the ability to learn from past experiences and apply them to new situations, sometimes even saving lives in the process. After my patient's battle with breast cancer, I became more aware of the importance of early detection and the unpredictable nature of the disease. This awareness shaped how I approached patient conversations, particularly regarding preventive screenings.

Nicole's Story

Another patient, Nicole, a forty-five-year-old woman, planned to leave the state for the summer to work on a short-term project. She was not going to get her mammogram before leaving, even though she was due for one. Nicole insisted there was no risk, citing her older sisters in Canada, who hadn't had mammograms due to different standards of care in their country. Screening after the age of fifty was the standard in Canada. She thought if her sisters were fine, so was she. However, I couldn't shake the thought of Clara and the late detection's impact on her life. So, I pushed harder, explaining the risks and the peace of mind that could come with getting screened before her trip.

After much persuasion, she agreed.

The result was devastating and lifesaving; Nicole had breast cancer.

Once Nicole shared the news with her sisters, they scheduled their mammograms, and both were diagnosed with breast cancer as well. Because of one conversation, we uncovered a silent threat affecting three women. More than that, their daughters who carried the gene would screen early, be more diligent about minimizing risks, and choose different forms of contraception.

This experience reinforced the notion that medicine is inherently uncertain, despite its scientific foundations. It's an ever-evolving practice where intuition, experience, and perseverance often play as significant a role as protocols and guidelines. Knowledge from one patient's story saved the lives of three others.

As I continue to learn from each patient, I'm reminded that while we follow standards, they are not set in stone. Medicine is constantly adapting, and so must we as providers.

The art of medicine has evolving standards and practices, which we apply as we continue to learn. Our care for patients is no different.

CHAPTER 17

Twenty Years with David

Of course, not all patients are as receptive to my feedback as I'd like. I don't think patients fully grasp the profound responsibility doctors carry when a patient opts not to follow their advice, particularly if the patient suffers as a result.

I first met David when he was thirty-eight. He walked into my office late, a Starbucks in one hand, and the scent of cigarettes trailed behind him like a second skin. He offered a half-smile and slumped into the chair as if he had somewhere better to be.

"Let's make this quick, Doc. My wife already told me what you're gonna say."

I reviewed his chart: Smoker. Overweight. BP borderline high. No time for exercise.

"David, you tell me; how do you feel?"

"Fine. Just tired, but that's life, right? Two kids, work, no time for anything else."

I observed him closely. He wasn't combative but detached, as if his health wasn't real. Maybe it was too much for him to process at one time, or perhaps he saw it as a distant thing, someone else's problem.

"You're headed toward chronic illness, David. This path leads to things you don't want, like heart disease, diabetes, and kidney failure. You may feel fine now, but this is the calm before the storm."

He chuckled. "Doc, everyone's got something. I'm too busy to worry about it."

That day, I tried to plant the seeds of small changes, such as quitting smoking, exercising more, and occasionally eating healthy meals at home. I gave him handouts and offered support. I felt calm, patient, and hopeful.

He listened, took the information I offered, and left, but he didn't change.

Two Years Later

David's next visit revealed that his blood pressure had increased, and his lab results indicated prediabetes. The appointment had been scheduled so I could go over his results and hopefully convince him to make changes to reverse the damage while there was still time.

"David, your lab results are a warning sign. You are lucky that you didn't wait; the results showed that you have diabetes. Prediabetes is a threshold that you can choose not to step over by changing eating and exercise habits. You can stop this." I encouraged.

"Come on, Doc. Prediabetes? Sounds like you're reaching."

"It's not a scare tactic. It's a warning. You can turn this around, but it won't happen by accident."

We discussed food choices, activity, and nicotine. I even offered smoking cessation resources once more. He nodded politely and lit a cigarette as soon as he exited the building.

Five Years In

David did not implement any of the suggestions I'd given him during his last visit. I'd seen this story unfold time and time again when patients did not heed my warnings. Breaking this kind of news to my patients never got easy.

"David, your lab results revealed that you have Type 2 diabetes. I'm sorry."

"Okay," he said, defeated. "What now?"

"We start meds, but David, this isn't just a medication issue. This is about reclaiming your health. Your life. I need you to meet me halfway because I can't do this for you."

"I can't promise anything, Doc. I'm exhausted. I work, I come home, I crash. And honestly? I don't see the point anymore."

"You are the point, David. You. Your life and health matter to your family and me."

David shrugged and stared at the floor as if he had no agency in the matter.

I left the room that day with a heaviness and a creeping fear. Am I losing him? Not just medically, but emotionally and psychologically. I saw the downward slope, and he didn't seem to care that he was on it.

Year Ten

Five years later, David arrived at my office complaining of lower back pain. He had gained more weight, gone to PT, and seen the pharmacist, but no sustained change had occurred. I saw frustration and defeat in his posture and eyes. How could I influence him to turn his health around?

"David, we've talked about this for years. What do you need from me that I'm not giving?" I asked gently.

"Nothing, Doc. It's not you. I'm just not built for this. I'm tired of fighting something I can't see."

The defeat echoed in his voice, setting off a cascade of doubts about my role in his decline. As his physician, I was engulfed by clinical frustration, yet it was the emotional weight that truly bore down on me. I couldn't shake the gnawing feeling that I was failing him. Had all my years of guidance and careful counsel been in vain?

Year Fifteen: The Heart Attack

David called me from the hospital. "You were right," he said, his voice unsteady. "I thought I was fine. Until I wasn't."

I froze. All those years of nudging, encouraging, and sometimes pleading with David to take his health seriously flooded my mind. There was always a family emergency, a stressful week, a birthday, or a barbecue. He had a gift for rationalizing his choices, and I had grown used to the tug-of-war between what he knew he needed to do and what he was willing to change.

I desperately hoped this would be the wake-up call he needed to change.

I visited him in the cardiac unit the next day. The beeping monitors, the smell of antiseptic, the weary look on his face—none of it shocked me as much as the look in his eyes. For the first time, I saw what had been missing all these years. Fear. Real fear.

"Let's not waste this second chance," I told him quietly, sitting beside his bed. "This is the moment we make it count."

He nodded, and for a while, he meant it. He threw out his cigarettes. We worked out a plan with small, realistic steps. He even started journaling, something I'd recommended for managing stress. For two weeks, he was steady.

Then life came crashing in, as it always seemed to do. A fight at home. A bad day at work. A moment of weakness. The streak ended with a single cigarette, then another, and soon, he was back where he started.

On his next follow-up visit, he sat across from me, sheepish but resigned. I went through the motions, adjusted his medications, and revisited our goals, but inside, I felt that familiar ache. A helpless, hollow ache from caring deeply and watching someone choose the thing that might destroy them.

After he left, I sat at my desk for a long time, staring at the corner of the wall where the light hit just right. My hands rested on the file I had updated for years; its pages were worn softly from use.

What am I missing? I whispered to no one. What else can I do?

Year Seventeen: The Amputation

Despite facing numerous health challenges, David remained largely unaware of an ulcer on the bottom of his foot that troubled him. For individuals with diabetes, we always recommend regularly checking their feet and getting an annual foot exam, as bacteria thrive in high-sugar environments. His blood sugar was extremely high, making him an ideal host for infection.

The ulcer got worse, and to complicate things, his work boot created another pressure point on his shin, which also got infected. The infection spread to both areas. We tried oral and IV antibiotics for nearly a month, but they didn't work. His blood sugar was too high, and the infection spread faster than the medicine could control it. He ended up needing urgent surgery.

Compounding this struggle were issues such as neuropathy and poor circulation, alongside the difficulty of managing uncontrolled blood sugar levels. These conditions painted a complex picture of his overall health, emphasizing a critical need for attention and care.

"I'm losing my leg?" he asked, his voice hollow.

"We tried, David. But your body can't fight infection when it's drowning in glucose. This is our best shot at keeping you alive."

He cried, the sound raw and unfiltered, echoing against the walls of the quiet room. I sat beside him, attempting to provide comforting warmth in the shadow of our shared grief. There were no platitudes to offer, no convenient solutions hidden in the folds of a lecture or pamphlet.

A thick blanket of silence enveloped us, heavy yet somehow comforting. Presence was all that mattered in that moment, my unwavering support, the steady rhythm of my breath beside his. His tears fell like raindrops on parched earth, and I knew words would only disrupt this sacred space we had carved out together. So, I sat with him, allowing the silence to speak volumes, the unsaid binding us closer in this fragile moment of vulnerability.

Year Eighteen

The amputation changed something in David. It was as if a switch flipped. He tried harder by using nicotine patches, sleeping with the CPAP every night, and preparing healthier meals. I saw glimmers of effort where there had been only resistance or defeat before. It was the most consistent stretch of follow-through I had seen in years.

Still, the damage lingered. Losing his leg meant losing his job. He had always taken pride in providing, moving, and doing. Now he was stalled. The depression settled in quietly, masked by fatigue and silence. Then it grew heavy, and he was tired all the time. He sat in my office with slumped shoulders, eyes dim, still grappling with habits he had spent a lifetime constructing like scaffolding around his identity.

"Do you think I'm a lost cause, Doc?" he asked one day, his voice low.

Something twisted inside me. I wanted to reach across the desk and shake the hopelessness out of him. I wanted to say no without hesitation, to give him a definitive path forward, but the truth was more complicated. I had walked with him for so many years, watching the slow unraveling of his health, the near misses, and the promises to do better. We ran out of room for delay.

I swallowed hard. "No," I said finally. "I don't think you're a lost cause. I think we lost time, and time matters."

Year Twenty . . . Now at 58.

David required dialysis three times a week. He had lost a leg to complications from diabetes. He suffered from diabetic neuropathy and coronary artery disease. His body was failing him in layers, and he knew it. The exhaustion showed in his eyes, but the regret in his voice stayed with me.

Did I fail? I sit with this question more often than I like to admit.

I can recall every moment over the past two decades—every plea I made on his behalf, every educational handout I placed in his hands, every honest conversation where I balanced encouragement with hard truth. I think about the appointments where I hoped something I said would finally take root, where I walked into the room carrying hope in one hand and realism in the other, hoping both would be enough.

It takes a toll, caring that long for someone and watching their health decline anyway. At first, I told myself I was being patient. Over time, I realized I was weary. Disappointment gave way to guilt, which gave way to anger, at the system, at his choices, sometimes even at myself. I felt helpless more often than I felt effective. I began measuring my success by my patients' outcomes, and when David's outcomes matched every fear I had tried to prevent, it felt like a personal loss.

I now understand, with some difficulty, that the truth isn't so clear. I didn't fail David, at least not to my knowledge. I stood by him, wondering whether my presence was always helpful. Did I offer too much compassion and not enough challenge? Should I have drawn a harder line? Or would that have pushed him farther away?

I never turned him away. I met him where he was, even when he wasn't meeting himself. Some days, he showed up prepared and open. On other days, he refused to make eye contact. Through it all, I held the door open again and again. He and his wife returned for over twenty years, and I welcomed them, no matter how discouraged I felt.

I never saw David as someone who failed me. That thought never crossed my mind. He was human. He was doing the best he could with the tools he had. He was scared, stuck, and suffering. That's what I saw. And while many systems failed him, like insurance gaps, socioeconomic barriers, and entrenched habits he could not quite shake, I stayed.

Maybe that's what medicine truly is. Not rescue. Not miracle-working. Just presence. A steady, stubborn kind of care that doesn't give up, even when nothing seems to change.

David is still here. He's still trying, in his imperfect way. So am I. Maybe that's not the outcome I had hoped for all those years ago. Still, it is not a failure. It is care. It is love, expressed through years of unwavering attention; perhaps, more than anything else, that is what it means to be a doctor.

CHAPTER 18

Wrinkles Are Not Bad

After a long day at the clinic, I was reviewing my schedule when Jean, an adult female patient, arrived for her appointment. In her late thirties, she was an energetic woman who took great pride in her appearance. Today, however, she wore a frown that hinted at her growing frustration. After exchanging pleasantries, I gestured for her to take a seat.

"I'm so glad to see you, but I'm really frustrated," she began, her voice tinged with urgency. "I've been researching Botox treatments to reduce these wrinkles, but my insurance won't cover it. I feel like I'm being denied something that could boost my confidence and make me more attractive to my partner."

I listened closely, understanding that her feelings stemmed from a deeper need for self-esteem. "I can see how much this means to you, Jean. Wanting to feel good about yourself is completely valid. Let's discuss the options available to you."

Jean took a deep breath and leaned forward, her eyes wide with hope. "I just don't understand why they won't cover it. It feels like they're saying I can't take care of myself or look how I want to look."

I gently explained, "Botox is categorized as a cosmetic procedure, which is why many insurance plans do not cover it. It's understandable to want a youthful appearance, but it's also important to recognize the distinction between medically necessary treatments and cosmetic enhancements."

Her expression softened, but I could see the disappointment still hanging in the air. "So, you're saying there's nothing I can do?"

I shook my head, trying to redirect her focus. "Not necessarily. While your insurance may not cover Botox, other options exist to address your concerns about aging and self-image. I believe it's important for us to explore the underlying emotions connected to how you view yourself."

Jean looked puzzled but intrigued. "What do you mean?"

"Sometimes our desire to change our appearance is shaped by societal standards or personal expectations," I explained. "It may be beneficial to talk to a therapist about how you view your body and what aging means to you. They can offer a supportive environment to explore those feelings."

She considered my words, her frown relaxing into a softer expression. "I've never thought about it that way. I guess I just want to feel attractive, especially for my partner."

"Feeling attractive is important," I affirmed. "However, it's also worth reflecting on what that means to you and how your self-worth might be tied to those external perceptions. Engaging in conversations about body image can sometimes reveal deeper insecurities and help you find confidence that isn't solely based on appearance."

Jean's eyes glimmered with understanding. "So, you're saying that rather than just focusing on fixing the wrinkles, I should think about my overall self-image and how I feel about myself?"

"Exactly," I replied, glad to see her warming up to the idea. "By tackling those feelings head-on, you may discover that your confidence grows in ways you hadn't expected. It's not only about the physical changes but also about your overall self-perception."

As our conversation continued, I shared resources for therapists specializing in body image and self-esteem. Jean's posture relaxed as she imagined a broader perspective on her self-worth.

"I truly appreciate this discussion," she said, a small smile breaking through her earlier frustration. "I've always believed I needed to look a certain way to find happiness. This approach is different from what I anticipated, but it might be just what I need."

As our appointment concluded, I reminded her that enhancing her self-image would positively affect her overall well-being. "You deserve to feel confident and valued, both inside and out. Working with a therapist could be a powerful way to support your journey."

Jean appeared lighter as she walked out of the clinic that day; her previous frustration had transformed into a sense of hope. I was grateful for the chance to guide her toward a more holistic perspective on self-acceptance and confidence.

While cosmetic procedures may offer temporary relief, the journey toward self-love and acceptance often necessitates deeper exploration. Don't get me wrong; Jean used Retin A creams and wore more hats to slow the wrinkling process. She may still move forward with cosmetic Botox but with a different attitude toward herself.

I wanted Jean to find the support she needed, and our conversation empowered her to embrace her beauty inside and out.

SECTION 4

Family and Relationships

CHAPTER 19

Wife and Mom

When Ella and her husband had young children, her days were a nonstop cycle of managing responsibilities that seemed to multiply. She'd wake up at dawn each morning, pack lunches, make breakfast, and coax everyone through their morning routines. After the kids were off to school, Ella's day was filled with paying bills, coordinating medical appointments for her parents, and ensuring their schedules didn't overlap with her kids' activities. She vented to her friends and me, her provider.

In the afternoon, she shuttled the kids to soccer practices, swim lessons, and skating, chatting with other parents and coaches to stay up to date on team schedules and upcoming events. She volunteered at the school, assisted with math enrichment in the classroom, and organized bake sales. When evenings came even after her husband returned from his long workdays, she often still had hours of helping with homework ahead of her, packing lunches for the next day, paying bills and answering emails. She would leave little time for herself to read or exercise, let alone time to spend time with her husband. Guilt did not overshadow all the tasks that remained on her list.

Then came the comments from her husband that were well-intentioned but gradually wore her down. After returning home to no dinner on the table after a hectic day, he'd say, "What did you do all day?" Or when his work project required longer hours, he'd tease, "Lucky you're at home. You've got it made!"

These words struck a painful nerve, leaving Ella feeling unseen and demoralized. She never told him. Instead, she internalized that she was not good enough or doing enough. These feelings deepened and became how she saw herself in the mirror daily. I once again told her that she was a beautiful person and that she played an essential and valuable role in the family dynamics. She needed to talk to her husband and tell him how she felt. I offered couples counseling, which she refused repeatedly.

One night, after a particularly exhausting day, Ella knew it was time to help him understand. She sat down with him and outlined the day's tasks, not to make him feel guilty but to provide a clear picture of her day. She explained how she ensured the kids started their day with breakfast every morning, cleaned up all the dishes from the sink, dressed the children, and got them out the door. Then, she managed errands and schedules that kept the entire family running smoothly. She shared the mental burden of remembering school deadlines, organizing activities, and ensuring their kids had the right gear for every event. And when their parents needed extra care, she handled appointments and assisted with groceries, all while keeping her commitment to stay healthy and recharged.

Her husband realized that while he was at work managing projects and meetings, she attended to their family's emotional and physical needs daily. Ella explained that she, too, was bearing a heavy load, even though it didn't come with a paycheck or regular performance reviews. The difference, she gently pointed out, was that she didn't have the luxury of calling her day "over" at five o'clock. Her "job" only ended when the kids were tucked in and the house was quiet.

As they continued their conversation, he realized that his comments, "Lucky you're at home," and "Didn't you get a break today?" had unintentionally hurt her, making her feel that her work was somehow less valuable. This open discussion prompted him to reflect on his assumptions and appreciate her contributions in a way he hadn't before. He understood that her days were a delicate balancing act, an endless list of visible and invisible tasks that kept their family afloat and thriving.

Gradually, their relationship grew stronger, and they started couples counseling. Her husband assisted with bedtime routines, made dinner on weekends, especially in the summer when he loved grilling, and handled soccer practices early Saturday mornings so Ella had time to recharge. She noticed his increased respect through these small gestures and his acknowledgment of the many roles she played. They regularly checked in with each other about their workloads, dividing tasks to ease each other's burdens. She also learned that her approach to tasks didn't have to match his, and she appreciated him for his support.

Through honest, patient communication, Ella's husband gained a new perspective, recognizing the profound impact of her work on their family's stability and happiness. This shift was transformative for Ella; it made her feel appreciated and showed her that their relationship was stronger because they understood each other's contributions. They became a united team, each taking pride in their roles and supporting one another, knowing their work was equally essential. Together, they created a balanced family life that allowed them to feel respected, understood, and valued.

As a physician, I value communication in every setting, both at home and at work. We don't have the TV on or phones at the table during dinner, and my husband initiates this exchange every night: "Tell me three things that you learned today."

There are no rules about the answer. It could be positive, negative, or a struggle that no one knew about. We seek connection by taking five minutes each night to listen to each other's triumphs and struggles. Communication, not just talking but also hearing, establishes trust and connection in my personal and professional relationships.

CHAPTER 20

Same Family, Different Holiday Cultures

When the holiday season rolled around for my friend Kate and her brother Tom, they would bring their families together for a much-anticipated week. Between them, they had five kids, each with a unique, vibrant personality, and the excitement would bubble over. Every year, Kate and Tom focused on giving their kids an experience rooted in connection, laughter, and stories, regardless of the cultural celebrations they embraced.

With Kate's family celebrating Christmas and Tom's embracing Diwali, they blended their traditions, creating a unique celebration that honored both holidays. The first evening kicked off with Storytelling Night, a cherished tradition. They dimmed the lights, letting the glow from the fireplace and a few flickering candles cast cozy shadows around the room. Each child took turns sharing something special, from funny stories about school to beloved memories with their grandparents. While Tom recounted the excitement of lighting diyas during Diwali, Kate shared a funny Christmas memory. The kids felt the closeness of family traditions passed down through generations, learning that joy could be found in both celebrations and everyday moments.

The next day was dedicated to making handmade ornaments and rangoli designs for the tree and the home. With the table covered in pine cones, paints, and colored powders, the kids got to work crafting their creations. Clara, Tom's daughter, was particularly proud of her glittery star, declaring it the "topper" for the tree. Meanwhile, the kids collaborated on a beautiful rangoli design, learning about the significance of the intricate patterns that symbolize welcome and prosperity during the Diwali festival. As they created, Kate and Tom shared stories of their childhood decorations, reinforcing the value of combining their cultural traditions.

That night, Tom suggested a cousin sleepover. The kids piled into sleeping bags in the den, turning it into a holiday hideaway filled with giggles and whispers. They watched their favorite festive movies, shared secrets, and made up games long after bedtime. Kate and Tom smiled knowingly at each other, recalling their late nights as kids. It was a time for connection, reminding them of the importance of family bonds that transcended cultural differences.

The next evening, the family bundled up in hats, scarves, and mittens for a walk around the neighborhood to look at the holiday lights. They filled thermoses with hot cocoa and strolled the streets, "oohing" and "aahing" at every new house decked out in twinkling lights. The kids took turns guessing which lights were new, while Tom's son Max creatively made up stories about who lived in each house and what holiday magic they might have inside. The walk became an adventure, highlighting the shared joy of Christmas lights and Diwali decorations, where light symbolizes hope and joy.

The following day was set aside for making holiday cards for loved ones. Everyone gathered around the table with markers, stickers, and stamps, creating cards for grandparents, friends, and neighbors. Kate's son, Sam, made a card for his favorite teacher, filling it with heartfelt thanks, while Tom's youngest daughter, Lucy, created one for her cat, complete with tiny paw prints. It was a small gesture, but it filled the kids with joy, teaching them the value of expressing love and appreciation, no matter what the occasion.

Later that week, they enjoyed a family baking day, which was a whirlwind of flavors and laughter. They collaborated to create traditional Christmas cookies and festive Diwali sweets, such as gulab jamun and besan ladoo. Tom led the "bake-off," challenging everyone to decorate their cookies as creatively as possible. The room filled with delightful aromas and giggles as the kids experimented with sprinkles and icing, learning to appreciate the culinary delights of both cultures. The baking day became a tradition, reminding them that sharing food was a universal language of love and affection.

Kate and Tom planned a day of charity activities as part of giving back. Together, they prepared small gift bags with treats and essentials to deliver to a local shelter. They talked to the kids about caring for others, emphasizing that compassion was fundamental to every celebration. The experience resonated deeply, and the kids took turns adding little notes and drawings to the gift bags. It was a grounding moment, a reminder that the spirit of giving was a common thread woven through Christmas and Diwali.

Before the week ended, Kate and Tom helped the kids create a holiday time capsule. Each child added a small item: a tiny ornament, a favorite drawing, or a note about what they loved most about this holiday. They sealed it in a decorated box, promising to open it together in a few years. Creating this time capsule gave everyone a sense of connection and anticipation, reinforcing that family memories are priceless, regardless of one's cultural background.

Finally, they closed the week with a movie marathon night showcasing Christmas classics and heartwarming Diwali films. The kids voted on their favorites, and everyone piled onto the couch with popcorn, blankets, and mugs of hot cocoa. They laughed, sang along, and even teared up during a couple of the movies, reveling in the warmth of family and the joy of storytelling. It was the perfect way to wrap up a week filled with love, connection, and memories that honored both cultures.

On the last evening, Tom and Kate gathered everyone to talk about their favorite memories from the year. It was a quiet moment, one of gratitude and reflection. The kids shared stories of school, friends, and family adventures, while Kate and Tom expressed their appreciation for blending their traditions. These holiday celebrations weren't about the gifts, the food, or elaborate plans. They were about creating moments of joy and connection that would carry on, rooted deeply in the hearts of their family.

As the week ended, Kate and Tom looked at their kids, now cousins bonded as close as siblings, and felt the joy of a holiday celebrating togetherness. Each child carried a piece of both cultures, learning that the essence of family transcends traditions and embracing a tapestry of love beautifully woven through their shared experiences.

CHAPTER 21

Gender Differences Sometimes Matter

Sometimes, doing the right thing isn't about finding the perfect solution; it's about doing what's right. It's about pausing, listening, and creating space for perspectives that don't neatly fit into a single answer.

Andrew, a physician I knew, faced a dilemma that lingered with me longer than expected. One of his colleagues, Lindsay, a bright and hardworking individual, was nearing the end of her pregnancy. It was her weekend to take calls, and his colleague quietly suggested that one of the partners could cover for her.

There was tension in Andrew's voice when he told me about it. "Our nurse practitioner suggested one of us should cover on call for Lindsay. She's thirty-six weeks pregnant, and it's her weekend on call," he explained. "She figured one of us could take it for her so she wouldn't have to be on call."

I raised my eyebrows, sensing his unease. "So, are you going to cover for her?"

He shook his head. "I don't think it's my place to offer. She didn't ask directly. In our culture, if someone does ask for help, they make it up later. Lindsay didn't ask. I do not want her to feel like I think she is not capable just because she is pregnant."

I took a breath, choosing my words carefully. "Maybe it is not about her being capable. She is probably pushing herself to keep up because she is new. She does not want to be seen as a burden. In medicine, especially in specialties like yours, the culture is intense. Men still dominate it."

Andrew frowned. "We have never treated her differently. She works as hard as everyone else. She has not said a word about needing help."

"That might be exactly the problem," I said. "It is her first year there. She is already pushing through so much. You and your partners are all seasoned. You know the team dynamics. She is probably trying not to rock the boat. People often do that when they feel like they do not fully belong yet."

"She is not showing any signs of struggling," he replied. "If I offer to take her call, it might make her feel like I think she cannot handle it. Like I am implying she is weak."

"Or maybe," I suggested softly, "it would show her she does not have to do it alone. That her colleagues understand pregnancy brings challenges, and it is okay to accept help. Maybe this is about creating a culture where different circumstances are recognized without judgment."

Andrew looked down, thoughtful. "There has always been this unspoken rule that if someone covers, it gets paid back later."

I nodded. "That rule might be fair on paper. It does not account for the pressure she is carrying. Sometimes fair is not fair."

He crossed his arms, wrestling with it. "I do not want to come across as paternalistic. She has not asked. If I offer, it could make her feel singled out."

"I understand," I said. "You do not want to make assumptions about her needs. Microaggressions often come from a good place. Even when unintended, they can make people feel less than. If she struggles silently because she thinks she cannot ask, that too is a burden no one sees."

Andrew exhaled. "You really think it would make a difference if I volunteered?"

I leaned back, meeting his eyes. "It could. It would show her she is supported. It is not about questioning her capability. It is about creating a work environment where she does not have to carry everything alone."

Andrew stayed quiet, the weight of the conversation settling over us. His struggle was not lost on me. There were no easy answers. Only competing values that each deserved respect.

What stayed with me most was not Andrew's final decision. It was the fact that he listened. He opened his mind to a perspective different from his own, even when uncomfortable.

Later, I discussed this situation with my daughters. One agreed that Lindsay should have asked directly for help, and the other believed offering help would have been the right gesture of compassion.

I saw the complexity even more clearly through their eyes. These moments do not easily split into right and wrong. They exist somewhere between autonomy and support, strength and understanding.

I realized that real maturity is not measured by certainty. It is measured by the willingness to stay open, honor the weight of two good choices, and listen even when the path forward is not obvious. That dilemma reminded me that respect does not always mean staying silent or stepping in. Genuine respect is the willingness to question, reflect, and let empathy guide the conversation.

Each situation we face carries nuances, shaped by individual histories, invisible burdens, and private fears. No two moments are identical, even when they appear to be the same from the outside.

The truth about microaggressions is that they are real. They erode dignity in subtle ways, and they deserve our attention and care. We must remain mindful of how someone carrying unseen burdens might perceive our actions differently, even those rooted in kindness and goodwill.

At the same time, an unrelenting fear of doing the wrong thing can paralyze us into inaction. Worrying excessively about how support might be received can sometimes deprive people of the care they need most. When we allow the fear of missteps to outweigh the impulse to extend compassion, we risk reinforcing the same isolation we wish to dismantle.

Navigating these moments requires humility. It demands that we approach each person and each circumstance with openness rather than assumptions, remembering that no single rule fits every situation. Respect lies not in perfect execution, but in the willingness to remain present, listen carefully, and choose action or restraint with love, not fear, at the center.

The deeper work of equity and inclusion is not about finding formulas but about cultivating a culture of belonging. It is about nurturing relationships where asking, offering, and receiving are all safe acts. In that spirit, perhaps the goal is not to avoid every possible offense, but to build enough trust that when we reach out, even imperfectly, it is understood as an offering of solidarity, not judgment.

That kind of culture expands with compassion, relationships, and courage.

That day, I thought deeply about the culture of medicine. It became clear how much the field still clings to unspoken rules, often established when medicine was almost exclusively male-dominated. If women are expected to silently meet the same unyielding standards without acknowledging different challenges, that doesn't create an equitable environment; it only reinforces burnout. Pregnancy is a real, valid change in a woman's life that shouldn't require her to pretend nothing has changed.

The more I thought about it, the more I realized that by staying silent, male doctors might inadvertently be reinforcing a culture that pushes women to feel they must "do it all." The silence speaks loudly in a system that often fails to understand diversity, equity, and inclusion (DEI) in practical, day-to-day terms. Ignoring the need for work-life balance or failing to acknowledge gender-related needs only risks pushing people to the brink, and burnout is one of the heaviest costs of that system.

CHAPTER 22

Boundaries Are Bridges

Being a physician has shaped who I am, but being a mother has shaped my heart. For over a decade, I've been on the sidelines at my daughter's sports club, not as a family care physician, but simply as another mom with a folding chair and a bag of snacks. I've quietly volunteered, helping where possible, never mentioning my profession except to friends. Leadership is familiar, but I've always preferred to cheer from the background rather than take center stage. Some roles matter more than titles, and being present for my daughter has always been enough for me.

However, the exclusive attitude of the club's Board of Directors didn't take long to notice. Though they were all volunteers, the board members were aloof, and any suggestions from non-board parents were routinely dismissed. Initially, I brushed this off as typical organizational dynamics, focusing instead on the work I loved, organizing events, managing equipment, and supporting the club as a dependable helper. Still, it was disheartening when some of my thoughtful ideas were overlooked or even met with subtle condescension.

Some parents recognized my natural leadership abilities despite my attempts to remain in the background. Soon, word spread about my medical expertise, resulting in a sudden shift in how the board treated me. Suddenly, they began to value my opinion and consulted me when making decisions. I was uncomfortable with this change because I didn't want my background to create a hierarchy. I appreciate all contributions, regardless of a person's title or credentials, and I was vocal about ensuring that everyone's ideas received equal respect.

Eventually, my daughter sought additional training with a more competitive team, and the board was offended. Despite my assurances that we remained committed to their club's events, they viewed this choice as a betrayal. The board president subtly implied that my involvement was "unnecessary" if my daughter trained elsewhere. Soon after, board members reassigned my responsibilities and reduced my participation without explanation. What hurt most was realizing that the friendships I thought I'd built over the past decade may not have been as genuine as I'd believed. My relationships with board members now seemed conditional, given that I no longer met their expectations.

My daughter, noticing the change, felt the sting of exclusion. As she watched me struggle, she became disillusioned by how quickly friendships could sour.

I sat down with her and explained that people's reactions reveal more about their insecurities than anything else. "You're allowed to be proud of your goals," I reassured her, "no matter how others react."

This was an opportunity to teach my daughter resilience, a lesson I hadn't anticipated needing to introduce her to at fourteen.

Through this process, my daughter learned from my words and observed my actions. She noticed me gradually distancing myself from the board's exclusionary behavior and finding fulfillment among other parents who genuinely valued me. Watching me let go of old ties while maintaining my grace and integrity inspired her to do the same, and we supported each other as we grew beyond the sting of exclusion.

This experience challenged me on a deeply personal level, revealing that even as an expert in behavior, I still had lessons to learn. Years of working with patients had taught me empathy, patience, and forgiveness, but now, confronted with the harsh reality of conditional friendships, I had to learn these lessons anew. Forgiving meant letting go of my hurt and moving forward, even if I couldn't erase the disappointment. My daughter witnessed this evolution and admired my ability to grow, even as an adult.

Together, we let go of the pain and moved forward, choosing to surround ourselves with people who shared our values. This experience deepened my understanding of resilience, not just for my daughter but also for myself. I learned to forgive, release past expectations, and prioritize authenticity over acceptance. My daughter learned the importance of standing firm in one's worth, regardless of others' opinions.

Learning and growth never truly end. By modeling resilience for my daughter, I rediscovered my own and found strength in forgiveness and the courage to walk away from relationships that didn't honor me.

CHAPTER 23

Holding Down the Fort

Kara sat in her quiet living room, watching the rain create slow trails down the windowpane. The house felt unusually empty, even with her two children asleep in their rooms. Her husband, Mark, had been deployed to Afghanistan weeks earlier, and the weight of his absence settled on her shoulders like an invisible cloak. As a nurse practitioner, Kara knew how to manage stress under pressure. Yet, no training could prepare her for the daily tension of waiting, wondering if each message or call might be the last.

Every morning, Kara woke before dawn to pack lunches, check homework, and ensure that her teenage daughter, Christine, and younger son, Jake, were prepared for school. Jake, at seven, was a lively child, full of questions and energy. However, Christine had changed since Mark's deployment. At fourteen, she was dealing with the usual high school challenges, but recently, she had been acting out. She was often moody, had started talking back, and seemed to struggle academically. Kara knew her daughter missed her father, but this newfound defiance concerned her.

Her days at the clinic kept her mind engaged, yet her heart felt heavy. She worked long shifts caring for patients, including mothers, fathers, and children. Listening to their stories sometimes made her think that her burdens were lighter; other times, it intensified her longing for family dinners and quiet evenings, which felt like a distant memory. While caring for others, her thoughts often drifted to Mark, wondering if he had found a time to call, a safe place to rest, or even a hot meal.

I saw the strain on Kara's face as we sat together in my office one morning. She cradled her coffee cup with both hands, her shoulders slumped. I'd noticed the change in her over the past few months, the tension in her jaw, the way she sighed more than she smiled. Mark's deployment had taken its toll on the whole family, but Christine's behavior weighed most on Kara.

"She's been impossible lately," Kara said, her voice strained. "It's like she's searching for a fight. Curfew, school, even the minor things, she's resisting all of it." She rubbed her temple. "And now Jake's starting to act like her, too. Same attitude, same sass. It feels like I'm losing both of them."

"That's not unusual," I said carefully. "Teens don't always know how to navigate significant changes like this. Christine's likely feeling scared or abandoned, even if she can't express it."

Kara frowned. "I get that. I really do. But knowing it doesn't make it easier."

I set my notes aside and leaned in. "Have you considered therapy for Christine? It could help her process everything in a safe environment."

She hesitated. "I don't know. I feel like I should be able to fix this. I'm her mom."

"You don't have to fix it alone," I said. "Sometimes, giving her someone neutral to talk to can make all the difference."

Kara's eyes filled with tears. "I hate feeling like I'm not enough."

"You are enough," I said softly. "But even the best moms need help sometimes."

Kara nodded slowly, her fingers tightening around the cup. "Maybe you're right."

Kara's parents lived just a few miles away, and even though she was fiercely independent, she relied on them for help. Every Friday, her mom would bring dinner and stay for bedtime. Those were the nights Kara breathed a little easier, leaning into her mother's support, with simple gestures, a home-cooked meal, a shared laugh, or a moment of silence each serving as a reminder that she didn't have to carry her burden alone.

Christine's teachers had also noticed the changes. Once an A-student, she was now slipping in her grades, submitting assignments late or not at all. During a parent-teacher conference, one teacher gently suggested that Christine might need extra support due to her father's absence. Kara felt a pang of worry in her chest but decided to consult a counselor for advice on how to help Christine and prevent Jake from following a similar path.

When Kara mentioned therapy, Christine narrowed her eyes. "Why can't you just listen to me, Mom?" She crossed her arms over her chest, her face tight with anger.

Kara felt a pang of guilt. Had her exhaustion made her less available? Had Christine been seeking her attention without the words to express it?

Taking a breath, Kara softened her voice. "This isn't about my not listening," she said. "I just think it could be beneficial to have someone you can talk to, someone who isn't me. No judgment. No pressure."

Christine's scowl lingered for a moment before it faded. "Maybe," she said, her tone quieter now. A fragile sort of relief flickered behind her eyes. "I guess it wouldn't hurt to try."

Jake, still young and impressionable, had started to pick up on Christine's behavior, even rolling his eyes and muttering "whatever" when Kara asked him to complete simple tasks. She knew he was too young to understand fully, but she worried he was learning to cope by mirroring his sister's defiance. While focusing on Christine was crucial, Kara couldn't neglect Jake, who needed just as much consistency, love, and stability.

During rare quiet moments, Kara would be awake at night, burdened by endless thoughts, logistics, to-do lists, and worries about what could go wrong. She understood that the possibility of loss was part of life as a military spouse, but that didn't make it any easier. Each day tested her strength, patience, and hope. Every night, she prayed for Mark's safety, imagining him under the same stars, somewhere on the other side of the world.

The clinic team also became her unofficial family. We all recognized Kara's resilience but also understood that even the strongest people need a shoulder to lean on. I would offer to take her place when the kids were sick or check in during lunch, encouraging her to take a few minutes. These acts of kindness became Kara's small lifelines, helping her navigate each day as her heart bore the world's weight.

One weekend, she surprised Jake and Christine with a camping trip to a nearby park. She wanted to recreate some of the memories they'd made with Mark before his deployment, hoping to keep his presence alive in their lives. They hiked, roasted marshmallows, and watched the stars from the tent, just as they used to. But as she lay there next to her children, Kara felt the sharpness of his absence more than ever, and she blinked back tears in the quiet darkness.

Christine's therapy sessions gradually showed positive results. While her defiance didn't vanish overnight, she became less reactive and more open to conversation. Kara observed small changes, such as Christine joining her in the kitchen, where they would prepare meals in comfortable silence or discuss school. Seeing his sister soften, Jake also started to calm down, with his playful nature reemerging.

The weeks turned into months, and somehow, Kara found her rhythm. She divided her days between caring for her children, attending to patients, and managing the numerous small tasks that kept her life running smoothly. Some days were more challenging than others, like anniversaries, birthdays, and holidays. The holidays were particularly tough, with family gatherings feeling incomplete without Mark. However, Kara drew solace from her family's warmth and her children's laughter, finding strength in the love of those around her.

As time passed, Jake and Christine reflected on her resilience. Kara encouraged them to find joy in simple pleasures: a sunny day, a beloved story, and a homemade pizza night. She wanted them to grow up understanding that they could count on each other and were stronger than they realized. Although they missed their father deeply, they learned that his love was always with them, even from miles away.

Kara's fears didn't fade, but she learned to carry them with quiet determination. Each day, she lived with hope and dread, balancing the joyful routines she had created for her children with her constant worry about Mark's safety. His sporadic and brief letters became treasures she reread on the hardest days, clinging to his words as tightly as she would hold his hand if he were home.

The phone rang in the middle of one afternoon. Kara wiped her hands on her jeans and picked it up, already bracing herself.

"Mrs. Taylor?" a man's voice said.

"Yes." Her throat tightened.

"This is Sergeant Miller from Mark's base. I just wanted to inform you that Mark is safe. There was a close call earlier today, but he's fine."

Kara's breath caught. "Close call?"

"Yes, ma'am. I don't have all the details yet, but I wanted to let you know right away that he's okay."

"Thank you," Kara whispered.

After hanging up, Kara stood still in the kitchen, the refrigerator's hum the only sound in the room. She was familiar with these moments, the sharp edge of fear followed by empty relief. But this time, it felt different. It stirred something inside her.

She slid down to the floor, her back against the cabinets, and buried her face in her hands. The tears came fast, harder than they had in months. She hadn't realized how much she'd been holding in, how tightly she'd been wound, until that fragile sense of safety nearly shattered. She called me just to have someone with her as she cried.

As Mark's deployment neared its end, we all grew excited. Jake and Christine made a sign and hung it on the door: Welcome Home, Daddy! Each day it stayed there was a testament to their collective hope and love, a reminder that no distance could truly separate their family.

When Mark finally returned, we gathered to welcome him home. Seeing him reunite with his family brought joy to all of us who had supported Kara during his absence. As we celebrated, I watched Kara stand with pride, surrounded by family and colleagues who had rallied around her during this journey. It was a powerful reminder that it truly takes a village to raise a family and to help each other shoulder the hardships of life, especially for those with loved ones serving far away.

Kara glanced around, recognizing the faces of everyone who had stood by her through countless sleepless nights and worry-filled days. Holding Mark's hand, she felt immense gratitude for the support system that had kept her grounded. We were all proud of Mark and thankful for his service, bearing our hopes and anxieties for his safety. In that moment, Kara realized that even during the most challenging times, she and her family would never have to walk alone.

Health, Wellness, and Work-Life Integration

CHAPTER 24

Leadership Gaps

M edicine has always demanded resilience, but in recent years, it has demanded more. Long hours, relentless expectations, and unspoken fears of seeming weak left even the most passionate physicians feeling drained. As a leader, I saw this in metrics and faces, and it became clear. We needed a cultural shift that started with listening.

It began with Becky, an outstanding nurse practitioner.

She loved medicine but wanted to coach her daughter's soccer team. The thought of asking for Wednesdays off filled her with anxiety. Would it make her seem less dedicated? Would leadership judge her?

Becky took a breath and came to me. She shared what coaching meant to her, how it wasn't about stepping away from work but into another meaningful role in her life. I listened. Together with our clinic manager, we reviewed staffing and coverage needs. It turned out we could make it work.

That one "yes" changed everything. Becky thrived. Her daughter lit up every Wednesday at practice. In the clinic, Becky was more present, energized, and engaged. Her joy outside of work reignited her passion for the medical field. That ripple effect taught me a vital lesson. When we support our providers as whole people, their performance improves, not despite balance but because of it.

Becky's story opened the door for others.

Dr. Vidya had been carrying the invisible weight of caring for an aging parent while trying to be present for her children. For months, she quietly debated whether to request part-time work. When she finally approached me, her honesty was met with understanding by me and my team. She transitioned to a part-time schedule, and her relief was immediate. Not only did she show up more fully at home, but her focus and patient satisfaction also improved at work.

Dr. Sara, who worked with an OB provider, was on the verge of burnout. The emotional demands of delivering babies day and night left her feeling hollow. After speaking with colleagues and then with leadership, she transitioned into a more clinic-focused role. The result? A deeper connection with her patients and a version of Sara that was engaged, content, and thriving.

These women had different needs but shared a common fear of asking and hoping that someone would listen to them.

I have always encouraged open conversations in our team meetings. I made it clear that no suggestion was too unconventional, and there was no need too small. We discussed the toll that our work took. We laughed. We got vulnerable.

Dr. Vidya spoke up again, this time to the whole group, sharing how her part-time shift changed her life. Others followed. One talked about needing flexibility for school pickups, and another required time to care for a spouse with cancer. Dr. Sara spoke candidly about her decision to leave obstetrics. What emerged from those conversations were more than individual stories; they were seeds of change.

Ideas flowed. What if we had wellness days? I proposed days off for self-care that wouldn't count against vacation time. We weren't there yet, but we were moving toward it.

We began small with peer support groups, a provider book club, a potluck lunch, and small acts of care that reminded us we were human first. The result? Morale rose, and so did patient satisfaction. We were showing up for ourselves and each other.

We'd made progress, but for real change to last, we needed buy-in from upper leadership, so I told our stories to them. During a leadership meeting, I shared Becky's Wednesdays, Vidya's part-time success, and Sara's clinic transition. These weren't just anecdotes; they were evidence. By supporting the well-being of our physicians, we retained top talent, improved productivity, and enhanced patient care.

I urged them to see the long game. Financial outcomes matter, but investing in people also pays dividends of engagement, quality, and retention.

To my surprise and relief, they listened.

They approved funding for wellness initiatives, manager training, mental health resources, and team-building retreats. They acknowledged that the bottom line couldn't come at the cost of burnout. In doing so, they opened the door for culture-wide change.

Today, we're seeing the results: Burnout is down, patient satisfaction is up, and our workplace feels different. It's not perfect, but it is honest, connected, and human.

I've learned that leadership isn't about having all the answers. It's about creating space for others to speak. It's about believing that everyone benefits when we care for the caregivers.

We change the understanding of the practince of medicine, not with sweeping declarations, but with one "yes" at a time.

SECTION 6

Perception and Identity

CHAPTER 25

Swingers in the Neighborhood

As I entered the room for the appointment, I was greeted by a married couple, patients I had cared for over the years as their primary care provider.

This day was unique. There was a palpable hint of excitement over impending parenthood. As we settled into our usual routine, we discussed their plans to start a family, navigating the conversation around stopping birth control, dietary choices, and lifestyle adjustments.

The atmosphere was filled with anticipation as I reminded them about the importance of handwashing after managing their two cats' litter boxes to avoid the risk of toxoplasmosis. Their eagerness was evident, and in that moment, I felt a sense of fulfillment, knowing we were laying the foundation for their exciting journey into parenthood, one filled with hopes and the joyful chaos of new life.

About six weeks later, the wife unexpectedly scheduled a follow-up appointment with me, requesting STI testing. Considering our recent discussion about pregnancy planning, this caught me off guard. My immediate concern was that one of them might have been unfaithful.

My mind filled in the gaps. Was there a lapse in trust? And if so, what would this mean for their plans to have a child?

Her unease was evident as her eyes shifted away from me, and her posture was rigid.

I reminded myself to remain open and nonjudgmental and asked her, "Good to see you again. What brings you in today?"

She responded tersely, "I need an STI test."

I gently probed, "Are there any relationship concerns you would feel comfortable discussing with me or a counselor? I can discreetly refer you."

She inhaled and glanced at me hesitantly, struggling to share more. After a long pause, she revealed something that surprised me. "My husband and I are members of a swingers group. There are six couples, including us. We just found out that recently, one of the members had an encounter outside of our agreed-upon group, and they contracted an STI."

She grimaced and continued, "Now, all of us must be tested as a precaution." She lowered her gaze after she finished.

Surprise flashed through me. This was a situation I hadn't considered, even though I had known them for so long. They had always been the quintessential married couple, and I had never once considered asking about non-monogamous practices, especially given our recent conversations about having a child. My shock faded as I recognized how vulnerable she must have felt sharing this with me.

I gathered my thoughts, "I respect your honesty and appreciate your openness. I want to emphasize that the choices you and your husband make are yours to decide, and my role is to support you without judgment." As I spoke, her shoulders relaxed, and her expression shifted to relief.

To ease any lingering tension, I talked about protective practices and reminded her of precautions to prevent conception with other partners. We also emphasized the importance of regular testing in these situations, as having multiple partners can increase the risk of exposure.

Reflecting on the encounter afterward, I realized I had unconsciously confined them to an image that matched my assumptions about what a married couple should look like. Although I had always prided myself on being open-minded and inquiring broadly about sexual activity, male, female, or both, I had never thought of mentioning non-monogamous practices unless prompted.

This experience served as a wake-up call, reinforcing the importance of setting aside assumptions, regardless of how well I thought I knew my patients. It reminded me to proactively create a safe space for patients to share their stories and practices, no matter how they defined their relationships.

I also noticed that my patient's trust in me grew due to my acceptance, which made her feel safe to be honest.

Since then, I have been committed to asking questions more openly and not projecting my assumptions onto others.

Every patient has a unique story. My role is to meet them where they are, respecting their choices while providing the care they deserve.

CHAPTER 26

Parenthood, Rewritten

Katie's desire to start a family was a quiet force, steady and unyielding, even when the odds were stacked against her. She came to me in her early adulthood, frustrated by irregular cycles and the nagging sense that something wasn't right. When she shared her dream of becoming a mother, I heard the hope threaded through her words, even as uncertainty shadowed her face. After her diagnosis of polycystic ovarian syndrome, we explored treatments, and I referred her to a gynecologist for more specialized care. They crafted a plan to manage her symptoms and improve her chances of conception, but the road ahead would not be easy. Still, Katie's resilience never wavered.

As time passed, she and her partner chose to pursue IUI and later IVF. Both processes took a physical and emotional toll on them, with each cycle bringing hope but ultimately leading to disappointment. I recall how deeply she felt with each failed attempt, yet she always returned with renewed determination to continue. Her strength was inspiring, even as she expressed her fears that her envisioned future might never be.

Eventually, after numerous conversations and introspection, she chose to pursue adoption. We discussed the steps she would need to take, and I was there to assist with some of the necessary paperwork and documentation, supporting her through each challenge as she embarked on this new journey. Watching her transition from the stress and heartbreak of fertility treatments to the hopeful anticipation of adoption was moving; she moved from despair to peace as she envisioned welcoming a child into her life.

The day she brought her child home was a moment of pure joy. She told me how her journey had given her a sense of wholeness she hadn't expected, and I could see how her family was finally complete. Her and her partner's love for their child was palpable, and in the years since, I have had the honor of caring for their family as it has grown and thrived.

This journey taught her and her husband about the various forms that love and family can take. Through the challenges of IUI and IVF, they learned the extent of their strength and resilience. They discovered how to support each other during tough days, growing closer and becoming more understanding of each other's hopes and fears. Although the process tested them, it also forged a deeper connection, strengthening their partnership in unexpected ways.

Choosing adoption taught them to let go of expectations and embrace life's unexpected paths. They realized that parenthood wasn't defined by biology, but by the commitment, care, and love they could provide. Bringing their adopted child home brought them a profound sense of peace, and they felt an overwhelming joy in finally becoming parents in a way that felt right and complete.

Reflecting on their journey, they often shared how much they had grown individually and collectively. They recognized that families can be formed in many ways and that the love they shared was more than sufficient to create a happy, fulfilling family. Their experiences brought them clarity and profound gratitude for one another and the family they managed to build against all odds.

There are many paths to parenthood, and support is crucial for each patient's unique vision of their family. Being part of her journey, from diagnosis to referrals and through the adoption process, reminded me of the diverse ways families are formed and the resilience of those who create them. It is a privilege to care for them as a family now, watching them grow together, each contributing to their beautiful story of love, patience, and joy.

CHAPTER 27

Breaking Generational Trauma

One of my patients, Dylan, came to me in his twenties, burdened by a deep sense of inadequacy and self-doubt. Much of it traced back to years of relentless comparisons to his father, who had towering expectations and little room for imperfection. Dylan had spent his youth striving to meet an impossible standard, leaving him feeling as if he was never quite enough, no matter what he accomplished.

When he began working with me, he confided a desire to reclaim his identity, to be proud of his accomplishments without chasing approval. His goals weren't abstract. He wanted peace. He wanted to feel whole without carrying the weight of someone else's definition of success. Together, we unpacked those layers. Therapy offered him the space to explore his emotions without shame. Medication eventually became a tool in his healing, too. For Dylan, accepting support initially felt foreign. He struggled with the notion that seeking help meant weakness. His courage, however, was evident in those quiet moments when he chose to keep going anyway.

In time, Dylan began to see himself more clearly. He noticed his quiet successes, the moments of compassion, the steady progress, and the values he had formed, despite, and perhaps because of, the pressure he had endured. He expressed a hope that stayed with me: to become a different kind of father. He envisioned a future where he could raise his children with support, respect, and love rather than fear and criticism.

Through Dylan's journey, I became both a student and a clinician. He showed me what resilience looks like from the inside out. His story reminded me that breaking free from generational patterns is never easy, yet always possible. Conversations about masculinity became moments of transformation, not just for him but for me as well. He taught me that healing often begins where expectations end.

By the time our work together ended, Dylan had embraced a new version of strength rooted in vulnerability, self-awareness, and authenticity. He no longer measured his worth by his father's shadow. He had learned to stand confidently in his light.

CHAPTER 28

Braver Than She Knew

In a bustling clinic filled with the hum of conversations and the faint rustle of papers, my seventeen-year-old patient, Mia, sat across from me. She bore the burden of a secret she had shared with no one. She had lied to her parents about being sexually active. Mia was in my office for STI testing, and her anxiety was palpable. I noticed the tension in her shoulders and how her hands fidgeted with the hem of her shirt.

"Hey, Mia," I said gently, offering a warm smile. "I want you to know that this is a safe space. You can talk to me about anything you're feeling or concerned about."

Mia hesitated, her gaze shifting to the floor before finally meeting my eyes. "I... I didn't want my parents to know. I thought it would be easier just to lie."

I nodded, acknowledging the fear and confusion in Mia's voice. "I understand. Many young people feel pressured to hide things from their parents, but it's important to discuss these issues, especially regarding your health."

Mia sat with her arms crossed, her gaze locked on the floor. After a prolonged silence, her voice finally pierced the tension.

"I'm scared," she whispered, her voice barely audible.

"Scared of what?" I asked gently.

Her eyes flicked toward me, then back down. "Getting pregnant. Or... worse." She swallowed hard. "I don't always feel like I have a choice And sometimes I think... maybe it's my fault."

"It's not your fault," I assured her.

She hesitated, her hands twisting in her lap. "I just can't tell my mom. She'd freak out. She'd probably think I'm disgusting or that I'm..." Mia trailed off, shaking her head. "She already barely trusts me. If she knew..."

"It's never too late to start a conversation," I said optimistically. "Honesty can be intimidating, but it can foster understanding and support. You deserve to have a trusting relationship with your mom."

Mia's eyes glistened with tears. "But what if she hates me?"

I leaned in slightly. "What if she doesn't?"

Mia's brow furrowed as she stared at her hands in her lap. After a long pause, she whispered, "Maybe, but I don't know how to start."

"You don't have to face this alone," I said. "Would you like me to be there when you tell her?"

Mia hesitated, then gave a slight nod. "Yeah. I think that would help."

A short while later, Mia's mom arrived at the clinic, her eyes scanning the room with quiet concern. She sat beside Mia, her hand brushing against her daughter's knee.

"Is everything okay?" her mom asked.

Mia's gaze flicked toward me, then back down. I gave her a small, encouraging smile.

"Mom," Mia's voice was shaky. "There's something I need to tell you."

Her mom's eyes softened. "Okay. I'm listening."

Mia swallowed hard. "I've... I've been seeing someone. It's serious. I'm, uh, I'm here to get tested for, you know, STIs. I was scared to tell you because I thought you'd be mad."

Mia's mom listened intently, her expression shifting from confusion to heartbreak. Tears filled her eyes as she realized Mia had been afraid to be honest with her. "I must have done something wrong," she said, her voice choked with emotion. "Why didn't you feel like you could talk to me?"

I intervened respectfully, reminding them, "This isn't about blaming anyone. Mistakes happen, and they're a natural part of learning and growth. What matters now is that you're both here, ready to have an open conversation."

Tears welled up in Mia's eyes. "I just didn't want you to be disappointed. I thought you'd be angry or think I wasn't responsible."

Her mom's hand tightened around hers. "Honey, I wish you had told me sooner, but I'm glad you're telling me now. I'm not disappointed or angry; you took responsibility by coming here. I just want you to be safe."

Mia nodded, and her mom pulled her into a hug.

Relief washed over Mia's face as her mom whispered, "I love you, no matter what. I want you to feel safe talking to me about anything, Mia. I don't want you to be afraid. We can figure this out together."

As the discussion continued, they explored ways to communicate better in the future. Mia learned that being vulnerable could foster deeper trust, while her mom recognized that open dialogue was essential for understanding her daughter's world. The clinic became a sanctuary for both, where mistakes turned into lessons and fears were met with love and compassion.

After the STI testing was complete, I talked with Mia about treatment options and ways for her to protect herself in the future.

Mia looked relieved and grateful for the supportive environment that had allowed her to be honest. "Thank you for helping me," she said. "I feel like I can trust you."

With renewed hope, Mia and her mom left the clinic, ready to embark on a new approach to their relationship, one built on openness and understanding. They were no longer defined by fear or mistakes but by their willingness to grow together.

The experience taught them valuable lessons: Honesty fosters connection, and errors can lead to healing, growth, and stronger relationships.

Reflection

Looking back on my journey as a family medicine provider, a mother of three, a first-generation female professional, and now a fifty-plus-year-old, I see a life shaped by resilience, compassion, and growth. Each experience, whether in the clinic, at home, or within myself, has taught me invaluable lessons about perseverance, empathy, and the delicate balance between caring for others and myself.

I have learned to see beyond diagnoses and treatment plans through years of working with patients. I have come to understand the stories behind each person who walks into my office, appreciating the fears, struggles, and triumphs they carry. Medicine is not just about science; it is about connection, trust, and being present in the most vulnerable moments of another person's life. My patients have taught me as much as I have taught them, perhaps even more. They have shown me the strength of the human spirit, the resilience of families, and the beauty in small victories.

Balancing my career with motherhood has been one of my most significant challenges and rewarding achievements. Raising three children while dedicating myself to my profession required me to master time management, patience, and flexibility. There were moments of exhaustion and self-doubt when I questioned whether I was doing enough in either role. Yet, in those moments, I discovered an inner strength I never knew I had. I learned that perfection is an illusion, that love is expressed in presence rather than grand gestures, and that my children were learning just as much from my struggles as my successes.

As a first-generation female professional, I carried the weight of breaking barriers and forging a path for those who come after me. Sometimes I felt the pressure to prove myself, to show that I belonged in spaces that were not always welcoming. Over the years, I have found my voice, standing firm in my knowledge, experience, and worth. I have become an advocate, not only for my patients but for myself and other women navigating similar journeys.

At half a century of life, I recognize that growth never stops. I have learned to extend grace to myself, to embrace the imperfections, and to celebrate how far I have come. My journey is not just about medicine, motherhood, or professional achievements but about becoming a fuller, wiser, and more compassionate version of myself. As I move forward, I do so with gratitude for every challenge, every lesson, and every life I have had the privilege of touching.

This book is my way of sharing those lessons, not just as a memoir of my experiences, but as a guide for others walking a similar path. I want to reach fellow providers who, like me, may have struggled with self-doubt, burnout, or the relentless pursuit of perfection. I hope to remind them that they are not alone, that their work is valuable, and that giving themselves grace is just as important as giving it to their patients. Medicine is a journey, not just to heal others but to heal and understand ourselves.

If I had a reader in front of me, I would want them to walk away feeling seen, understood, and encouraged. I want them to know that growth is not about reaching a perfect endpoint, but about learning, evolving, and embracing the moments that shape us. Through these pages, I hope others may find validation, strength, and permission to be human in a profession that often demands so much from us. We are not just doctors, parents, or professionals; we are people, and that, in itself, is enough.

THE END